English Language

The Gateway to Global Growth

Chitra G. Lele

ATLANTIC

PUBLISHERS & DISTRIBUTORS (P) LTD

Published by

ATLANTIC

PUBLISHERS & DISTRIBUTORS (P) LTD

7/22, Ansari Road, Darya Ganj,
New Delhi-110002
Phones : +91-11-40775252, 23273880, 23275880, 23280451
Fax : +91-11-23285873
Web : www.atlanticbooks.com
E-mail : orders@atlanticbooks.com

Branch Office
5, Nallathambi Street, Wallajah Road,
Chennai-600002
Phones : +91-44-64611085, 32413319
E-mail : chennai@atlanticbooks.com

Printed in India at Nice Printing Press, A-33/3A, Site-IV, Industrial Area, Sahibabad, Ghaziabad, U.P.

Dedicated to

My guiding beacon of light,
My mother,
Mrs. Asha Lele.

Enriched minds,
New visions,
Great insights,
Learning opportunity,
Intelligence network,
Seamless culture, and
Huge payoffs.

—Chitra G. Lele

Learning is a treasure
that will follow its owner everywhere.

—Chinese Proverb

Foreword I

This inspirational and motivational book by the young author, Chitra Lele, makes a compelling case for studying English and offers many practical tips for effective and enjoyable learning.

English is a beautiful and highly expressive language with many forms. The parent form survives as South British English but other standards such as American English, Indian English, Australian English, and Scottish English—all preserve different historical features, or add their own innovations to enhance what is now a global language. This does not mean that other languages, particularly minority or regional languages should be threatened. As this book points out, our mother tongue is an important part of our identity and of our philosophy or world view. We think about and describe what the words of the language in which we are thinking permit. Our language determines how we see the world; when we become thoroughly familiar with another language our eyes are opened to a whole new way of seeing and interpreting the world. If you are reading this book, you must already know quite a lot of English. I hope Chitra Lele persuades you to persevere in broadening and deepening your knowledge of the language and its associated culture.

It has been my great privilege for many years to teach academic writing to postgraduate students at the University of Edinburgh and I have been greatly enriched by the different cultures, philosophies and attitudes to life that my students have brought, born out of languages from all over the globe and shared in the common ground of the English language. They have taught me, and each other, many things. We have much to share with each other, and having a common language is the first step along that road to engaging in commerce and scientific research and to sharing knowledge and friendship. Chitra's book reflects this very philosophy.

The book deals with global aspects of English like educational equity, cross-cultural sensitivity, seamless cohesion, etc., in a lively and stimulating manner.

If you can apply the ideas in this book in your everyday life, you will find that your confidence in using English is growing.

This book will help you achieve your goals!

Christine Robinson,
M.A., Ph.D.,
Honorary Fellow,
Linguistics and English Language,
University of Edinburgh and
Director of Scottish Language Dictionaries

Foreword II

Chitra Lele holds degrees in computer management and software engineering. As an author she is a record setter and has received letters of commendation from the President of India, Her Highness Queen Elizabeth and other prominent personalities. Her books include *The 6 Spheres of Life: Unlocking the Door to Success and Happiness* and *Organizational Democracy: Collaborative Team Culture: Key to Corporate Growth*. She is often invited as a keynote speaker and also as a management consultant. Amidst her hectic schedules, she manages to find time to build a network of peace ambassadors, and to apply her knowledge to bring freshness to various corners of life in her unique ways.

The young author came to my close attention when I was editing *An Interpretation of Stephen Gill's Mind and Art*. Those were hectic days for me because of the work relating to book editing, work at college, and invitations from Canada for readings and to receive an honor. That was the time when Chitra asked me to write a Foreword for her book *English Language: The Gateway to Global Growth*. I could not say no because I was impressed with her achievements and particularly with her contribution to my anthology. This happened a few months ago.

I find Chitra's book meaningful, particularly when the literary bazaar is swarming with materials that claim to be helpful to learners and learned. This book is another achievement of the young author that deserves to be brought to the attention of equally deserving readers because it is a volume that tells about the development of English language and its growing importance. This manuscript is a display of the material that inspires to master the skills of English.

The book is a gallery for the author to display her own interest in English. Chitra brings in the necessity of English that to her seems a door to the world of success. She is convinced that

English language can liberate a person from the confines of the boundaries. Language acquisition can be a pleasure and can also provide a refined delight to understand culture and literature. English undoubtedly is crucial in most fields, because it is a magnet to attract people also in the world of commerce, and is a shockproof cover against the shockwaves of globalization.

Through this book the author affirms her faith in shaping one's destiny according to one's own choice. She believes in the potential of a human being to be able to carve his/her name in a fearless fashion to move forward. I find this book meaningful because its illustrations have touched my heart and I am sure they are going to touch the hearts of many more. They also stir minds making them realize what they miss if they lack a proper knowledge to use the English language.

Languages may open new vistas for learners. The more languages one knows the better are the chances for progress. English provides a chance to develop in any field of one's choice. It helps one to grow. It does not confine a citizen to his or her own nation. It opens the possibilities to be global in the real sense.

Chitra's book is the result of the hard work, research, dedication and extensive experience. It contains samples which show the author's deep knowledge of the subject and concern for the people who do not know English. It is an enormously useful guide that gives an insight into the behavior and nature of English language. This book offers practical advice to beginners and also to those who know it well. The author has put her best to produce a book that has practical as well as aesthetic pleasure. It is useful for learners, learned, as well as for those who read just for delight.

I congratulate Chitra for writing this book. I bless her to keep on walking on her chosen path with more vigour to be able to produce more such works.

Dr. Anuradha Sharma,
Assistant Professor of English,
Associate, Indian Institute of Advanced Study, Shimla and
Recipient of Woman of the Year award
from *Bharat Times* (Canada)

Preface

English, as an entity, has gained stupendous importance in the last 50 years or so. Despite the rich tapestry of languages in the world, this is one language that stands out (or should I say it is outstanding).

English as a means of global communication, knowledge exchange and seamless cohesion is continuing to experience paradigm shifts. In present times, the world is a global classroom for English and you are a potential student in this classroom. Every person wants to learn and master English language. Learning and mastering English is not just limited to classroom experiences. The process is about encountering and instilling the values of a whole new culture. (This holds true for any language that you are planning to master.)

A few months ago, one of my friends narrated a life-changing incident to me. It was about his driver, who wanted to move on in life. My friend's driver was an intelligent man, who knew that his lack of knowledge of English language was the main barrier in the path to his progress. He was aware of his shortcomings, but what he was not aware of was how to remove them and move ahead. My friend, a symbol of positive progress, ensured that his driver got to live the life of his dreams because he himself had been through this process of transformation. He knew the benefits of this language and he is very much reaping the fruits of benefits till this very day. Now, isn't this an inspirational 'English' episode? No matter what you are doing in life—business, studying, training or globe-trotting, the point is to understand that English will benefit you in innumerable ways.

For the past several years, the American dream has been often lined with migration to the United States—the land of opportunity. To capitalize on this opportunity, one needs to be well-informed, not only in the way the natives eat, walk, dress, and celebrate, but also be familiar with how they communicate. This is where English steps in.

Just as the demand for Test of English as a Foreign Language (TOEFL) is growing, so is the demand for Teaching English as a Second Language (TESL) on the rise. In both cases, the current trends indicate that the supply cannot match the demand. These trends surely point towards a bright 'English' future.

The fierce rate at which English language courses and degrees are burgeoning in several universities across the world implies that we need to act now. We need to join in to capitalize on these trends.

Globalization is the main factor for the growing interest in English language coming from academic communities, both real and virtual. You need to be prepared, if you want to survive in a foreign land and be able to absorb the cultural shocks. With English on your side, these shocks are manifested into portals of unlimited possibility.

English serves as a unifying element in various facets of our lives. Let us all join in to strengthen this bond!

All the above points (and much more) are covered in detail in this book. The book is easy enough to navigate and is divided into three parts:

> Part I deals with the background and rich history of English. It also highlights the importance and relevance of English in this world in transition, in this era of economic modernization.
>
> Part II discusses the role of English in educational equity and in building a seamless culture. It also talks about the importance of English in various fields.
>
> Part III deals with how to learn and improve English. It demonstrates the power of linguistic tools through various exercises. It also deals with the future trends and the likely nature of English in the wired world. The book ends with the Bonus Bytes and Real Life Quotes chapters.

The chapters also include real life experiences, useful illustrations, insightful surveys, fun exercises, spotlight tips, worksheets and questions for reflection, which help to enhance our understanding of the importance of English in today's world of globalization. Appendices include some important acronyms and information on English language courses. I hope that my book will serve as a practical guide, and help you to relate the information shared herein to your individual contexts and personal experiences.

Chitra G. Lele

Acknowledgements

This book, while an individual work, benefited from the insights and direction of several people. I use this opportunity to express my heartfelt thanks to all those who supported me in one way or the other during the completion of this writing project.

What I have learned over the years comes as a result of being a daughter of wonderful parents—Mrs. Asha Lele and Mr. G.G. Lele. They have been the motivation that has helped me to maintain laser-sharp focus on my goals. Thanks to them for their on-going support, helpful criticism and valuable suggestions.

I owe my sincere gratitude to Dr. Christine Robinson for her helpful feedback, guidance and scholarly Foreword - I. Her extensive experience and insights have been enormously helpful in writing this book.

I am heartily thankful to Dr. Anuradha Sharma, whose encouragement and guidance from the initial to the final stage enabled me to complete the book successfully. Thanks to her for taking the time to write a wonderful Foreword - II to the book.

Very special thanks go out to the members of the Brainlines Team (www.brainlines.net) for their incredibly creative work on all the illustrations.

Without the generous help of the various professionals, students and teachers that I interviewed around the world, the compilation of statistics and key observations would not have been possible. I thank them all for their time and their patience shown towards me and my questionnaires, which in turn has produced interesting points and thought-provoking findings.

I thank all the contributors of the 'Real Life Quotes' chapter. It is because of these wonderful people that we get to learn some interesting facts about English.

I offer my deep gratitude to the Higher Essence for bestowing on me the strength to follow my heart. May His name be glorified, exalted and honored.

Last but not least, I am extremely grateful to the Atlantic team for their constructive comments and unflagging support. Their editorial feedback, design inputs and constant reviews have transformed this writing project into an informative and interesting book.

Chitra G. Lele

Contents

PART II: BEYOND THE BEGINNINGS

APPENDICES

List of Tables, Illustrations, Figures and Worksheets

A. List of Tables

B. List of Illustrations

C. List of Figures

D. List of Worksheets

PART-I

Globalization and the Growing Use of English Go Hand-in-Hand

1 Introduction—'Working Towards a Common Platform'

English is the gateway to opportunity;
It makes the road ahead less bumpy.

People produce written words and spoken languages on a continual basis, and the English language and its long running history is a product of such creative pursuits. English, which began 1600 years ago as a means of communication in the British Isles, now makes its presence felt in every nook and corner of the world. We have literature from the Old English period (such as the poem The Dream of the Rood) which shows that this was a linguistically and intellectually rich culture with a highly expressive language. Today, it is that common platform, through which we can share our life experiences and pursue the realization of a collective vision. It is the language of cultural modernity. English has been influenced, is being influenced and will continue to be influenced by a repertoire of experiences, both linguistic and non-linguistic in nature. No wonder, its influence on the world stage is increasing day by day. No wonder, it has become a major component of the world linguistic DNA.

The English language is a member of the Germanic family of languages. Germanic is a branch of the Indo-European language family. The word *English* first appears (as *englisc*) in the 10th century. This is from *engle* + the adjective forming suffix which appears in modern English as *-ish*.

According to research figures, English is used by around 400+ million native speakers, 350+ million non-native speakers, and there are another 300+ millions in the process of learning it.

Did you realize that over a billion people in the world are associated with English? After the Second World War, globalization catapulted the further spread of English thereby influencing the fields of education, arts, aviation, scholarship, entertainment, diplomacy, science and commerce. This spread also opened the doorway to migration opportunities.

In the post war period, the assimilation into English-oriented countries increased, particularly in the United States of America. Over the last 30-40 years, migration has encouraged the development of different varieties of English. The main reason for this is that in current times, not only economic factors are globalized and exchanged, but also cultural factors like music, arts, lifestyles, literature and languages are exchanged. This large-scale migration has resulted in new growth models, where the prospects of a better lifestyle and lucrative pay packages have motivated thousands of people to pursue English education. Global relocation can lead to global growth only through the gateway of English.

Spotlight

During my first visit to Lyon, France, I got a severe throat infection, and I had no choice but to consult a local doctor. I was in a big fix and I really did not know how to convey my problem to the doctor, as the only French words I knew (back then) were *adieu, bon appétit, merci* and a few others. (Now, I am in a much better position, when it comes to speaking the French language.) To my surprise and relief, the French doctor was really good at English. There you go, you will find English-speaking people on all points of the world compass.

At the height of the British regime, the British had a strong foothold in almost every part of the world. They carried out trade in practically every continent, and that is one of the main reasons for the widespread usage of English. Later on, when the Americans took over and their power overshadowed the British rule, there was no need for people to adopt a new language as Americans communicated in English too. This dual impact strengthened the status of English, all the more. Now, it is a powerful magnet of opportunity for one and all.

Apart from the impact of British colonization and Americanization on the world, one of the most inherent qualities of English is 'Internationalization' which makes it such a popular language. Due to the thinning of national borders, the world has now become a global village, all because of this versatile language, which is sweeping the world's social, political, economic, physical and virtual space.

From the late 15th century, the language changed into Modern English. English, which we all know, and which is greatly influenced by phonetic changes, something we all refer to as the 'Great Vowel Shift'.

Nowadays, English is referred to as 'International English', 'World English' or 'Global English'. English is no longer just a medium of bringing about cultural neutrality, but also about building a scientific and academic society. English is no more the intellectual and cultural property of the British. Most of the times, English is used as a *lingua franca* without the involvement of native speakers of English. This goes to show that English is not just theirs, yours or mine, but it is OURS. It is true that each one of us has 'a share in its ownership'. The main reason for people being more English-friendly is that they have realized holding linguistic biases only tends to thwart growth, both personal and professional.

1.1 The World in Transition—'The Role of English in this Transition'

In this world in transition,
It is always beneficial to be
English driven.

The 19th and 20th centuries played a critical role in establishing English as a global language. By the beginning of the 19th century, Britain had become a world power. The British colonialism spread its wings far and wide, thus making English 'the language on which the sun never sets'. By the end of the century, USA too had become a powerful force. Its dominance and economic supremacy was increasing, and was felt throughout the 20th century. First, the impact of British imperialism, and then the superpower of the US dollar, fuelled the establishment and expansion of the English language. This momentum continues even today as the walls between nations are being torn down.

Even after the end of the colonialism, what occurred on the linguistic front in nations which were freed from its clutches strengthened the position of English, even more. How? Well, these nations felt they could re-establish their lost identity by having their own official language. But most of them were in a dilemma because they had so many local languages to choose from and short-listing one was not possible. Thus, they had to continue using English.

Whatever our view of the world in transition is, we cannot think of it without a reference to the role played by English in this transition. Transition is about enhancement. And when we talk about this enhancement, we also need to strategize preparation for meeting the future challenges. One of the most critical components needed to prepare for the future is the power of information. In current times, people who possess this power are the ones who have good command of English.

If one knows how to communicate well in English, there is a greater chance to survive the shockwaves of the globalization movement. Its presence and growing influence is overwhelming. Whether you are an Indian student representing your country in an international education meet, or a businessman on a business trip in Manila, or a Chinese keynote speaker in Glasgow, you are probably communicating in English.

English is an important prop for playing your role well on the world stage. In other words, it provides the much needed competitive edge to emerge as a winner in the global race. In order to maintain this edge, it is imperative that we continue to improve our mastery of English. English plays a major role in technology's global triumph, and Asian countries like India with a large pool of English-speaking workforce have benefited a lot from this triumph. The geographical and domain reach of English is far greater than that of any other language.

English is used for more purposes than ever before. In global settings, English is used in both public and personal domains, and it functions as a language of wider communication.

Globalization impacts all conceivable areas of life and English plays a major role in this impact. It leads to "brain exchanges" and "sharing of global ideas" between countries thereby playing a major role in the information flows, and services and products chain. Hence, globalization and English are directly proportional to each other.

Most of the wonders of globalization that have been created over the last 100 years are by English-speaking people, and therefore everything related to the inventions is documented, explained and shared in English.

Within a few centuries, English has transitioned from an island tongue to a world language. English is the linguistic engine driving the wheels of globalization. Whether one converses with his/her family members or moves about to converse with others, he will not feel tongue-tied, if he has the knowledge of English.

> **Spotlight**
> Globalization is directly proportional to the spread of English.
> Effective communication in English is the key to riding high on success in this wave of globalization.

English is the virtual window of opportunity, helping to forge new collaboration links in terms of social ties and economic relations between nations.

1.2 The Background—'A Rich History'

Be it old, middle or modern English,
It has been, it is and it will continue to be
A language so very rich in history.

The English language has a long and interesting history. From humble beginnings to its modern day *avatar*, English has come a long way. Over the last 1600 years, it has evolved into a global phenomenon that we are experiencing today, which reigns supreme within the linguistic dynasty.

We all know English, but do we know where it comes from? The history of the language can be traced back to the Anglo-Saxon dialects in the 5th century A.D. It was brought to Britain by three Germanic tribes (Angles, Jutes and Saxons) from various parts of Denmark and northern Germany. The timeline of this language can be divided into three distinct phases:

(i) **The Old English Period (500-1100)**: Old English (also called Anglo-Saxon) is the ancestor of Middle English and Modern English. It survived for almost 700 years, right from the 5th century to sometime after the Norman Conquest.

(ii) **The Middle English Period (1100-1500)**: The period of Middle English begins with the Norman invasion of 1066 A.D. In this timeline, several changes affected the structure of this language. More stress was laid on word structure. It was heavily influenced by French and Latin after the Norman invasion. There was a great influx of French and Latin loanwords. Danish Viking invasions and the influence of Old Norse influenced English too. *Sky, skin, name, they, their, them, both* and many other common words are the result of the Viking invasion and settlement. There was a kind of linguistic division, where the upper class spoke French and the lower class used English. English regained prominence in Britain during the 14th century.

(iii) **The Modern English Period (1500-Present):** Here the period from 1500-1800 could be referred to as the period of Early Modern English, and anything and everything from 1800 onwards is Late Modern English.

The most prominent change in Early Modern English was that of the *Great Vowel Shift*. This resulted in a major change in pronunciation. Renaissance of classical learning and the British coming in contact with other nations led to the inclusion of many new words in the language. The invention of printing also played a major role in the spread and standardization of this language. The literacy rate in English rose as publishing of works in English became cheaper. All these historical events mark the separation of Middle from Modern English.

It is in the Late Modern English period that this language has developed the most. Vocabulary has expanded a lot due to

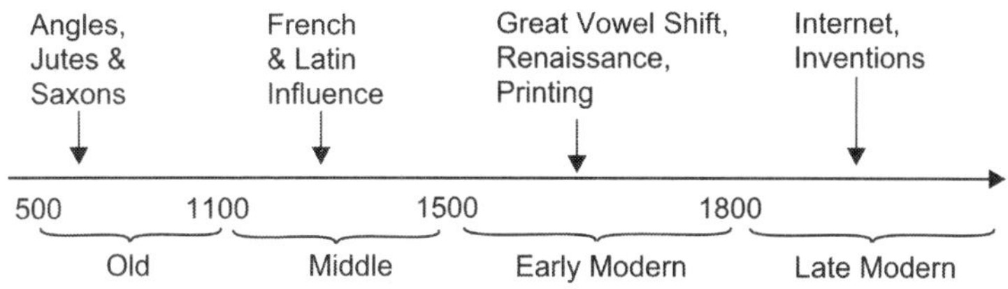

Figure 1.1: The English Language Timeline

new inventions, foreign words and the rise of the virtual empire of the Internet. The 19th and 20th centuries have seen a barrage of innovations hitting all domains, which kind of resulted in English becoming the primary choice of global awareness, expression and progress.

> **Spotlight**
> Interesting Tidbit
> Angle Land → Engla Land → England

It is interesting to note that the English-speaking areas have expanded at all periods of this timeline. If we start to cover the periods, we may end up writing an entire book. For the sake of understanding, it is necessary to cover the background of this language from the 15th century onwards.

From the latter part of the 15th century, the language changed into what we all know as Modern English. Modern English has been spoken since the Great Vowel Shift.

By the 1900s, the development of the English language took a giant step as a result of the Industrial Revolution, and subsequently due to the Technology Revolution. From the mid-20th century, the stronghold of English began to shift from British to American English. The economic aggressiveness of the United States of America has contributed to the further expansion and dominance of English in a globalizing economy.

Today, English is listed as the official or co-official language of over 90 countries, and is spoken extensively in other countries where it has no official status. The largest concentration of English speakers is found in United Kingdom, India, United States, Australia, Ireland and Canada. This is far more than the status achieved by any other language. Scholars frequently refer to its latest phase as World English.

We cannot forget that English, in itself, is a product of linguistic breeding of various influences of older languages like Latin and German. From the margins of Western Europe to all parts of the world is what English is all about. There is a remarkable variety based on sounds, pedagogical norms, spellings, grammar and vocabulary within the English-speaking world.

1.3 The Big Picture—'Let Us Paint the Success Story'

English is the nucleus
Of worldwide progress.
English is the canvas
On which we paint our success.

'English is the most widely spoken tongue', 'English is super great', 'English is your ticket to success', such lines are sprinkled all over in newspapers, digests, journals, pamphlets, hoardings, magazines and news channels. Why so? The reason is simple—no other language till date has been given such widespread coverage. It is not surprising that this language is always making headlines.

English has been given a special place, in one way or the other, in almost all parts of the global landscape. More than the number of people speaking this language or its literary power, what makes this language universal, is its 'special status' tag. Any language which has the following three usage areas—Mother tongue, Official language, and Second/Foreign language to it is a strong contender for the global language title, and this is exactly why English is the undeclared queen.

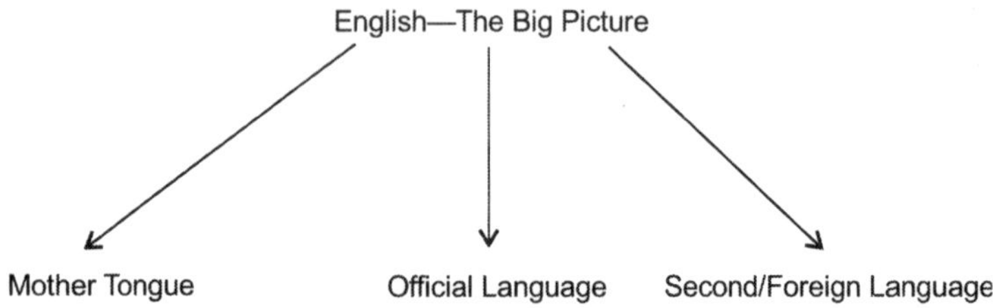

Figure 1.2: Special Status—The Big Picture

No other language has ever had such an everlasting impact on other languages, international trade, politics, international relations and world history. In current times, English has spread into many new domains, also into the more personal ones such as family, social networks and friends. This testifies for the increase in the functional significance of English communication.

English as a language performs diverse functions. It is often the difference between a life of a clerk working for a few dollars per day and an executive with a high-profile, progressive career in corporate fields like finance and IT. A high-level of English proficiency stands not only for a strong academic foundation and social success, but also provides links to the mainstream professional opportunities.

1.3.1 Importance of the English Language Survey

Attitudes and opinions are crucial in language growth or decay. People all over the world have realized the importance of English language acquisition.

(a) *Sampling design*

To study the opinions and attitudes of people towards English, I conducted a pilot study on a sample of 150 people from different cultures and professions, in the age range of 25 to 55, and with an experience base of 3 to 30 years. The respondents had varying levels of proficiency and academic achievements. These people were from countries like United Kingdom, France, Canada, India and the United States.

(b) Questionnaire

With regards to opinions and attitudes towards the language, a set of questions were asked about what the respondents felt regarding the use of and their attitude towards the language. These questions were related to the advantages of English.

(c) Results

These are my findings from the pilot study based conversations that I picked up with people on my visits to United Kingdom, France, Canada, India and the United States.

Factor	*Strongly Agree*	*Strongly Disagree*	*Don't Know*
Better career opportunities	146	2	2
Gain competitive edge over the others	148	0	2
Better interpersonal communication skills	142	4	4
For traveling abroad	145	3	2
For enhanced reading and writing competence	141	5	4
Improve the corpus of specialized terms and professional terminology	140	7	3
Compose accurate messages, reports, e-mails	145	3	2

Findings: From the above wealth of factors, it is evident that a large chunk from the sample of 150 people has positive orientation towards the English language. Over 97 per cent of the respondents perceive English as a means of tapping better career opportunities and also expressed the need of teaching this language at the very beginning of formal education. It has been reported by 94 per cent of the participants that they are encouraged by their colleagues, friends, classmates and family to constantly improve their English levels. Over 93 per cent of the respondents were of the opinion that Standard English is necessary to be intelligible internationally, especially in the corporate space.

Few respondents did express their concern about English and its widespread influence, but again, they said that they do not view this widespread influence as an invasion on their identity or a threat to their culture. One of the respondents had a very interesting take on this point; he said, "Any language, including English is a skill, which is neutral by nature. In that sense, the more language skills one possesses, the better are one's chances of progress and survival". My views totally resonate with this respondent's views—You can very well learn other languages, without severing the connection with your culture, ideological roots and the essence of your identity.

I strongly believe in being proficient, both in your mother tongue (in the case of non-native speakers) and in English. But these days, I see a sad trend where certain people tend to look down upon their mother tongue and abandon learning it completely, and only stick with English. They tend to take on a new accent and a new identity altogether. Any language, be it English or your mother tongue, is a *carrier of culture*. In the case of non-native English speakers, ignoring your mother tongue, in a way, is acting like a cultural atheist. Just as we connect with the global roots through English, you should take pride in the fact that your mother language is your route to your roots and a way of bonding with local communities. Learn English but not at the cost of losing the connection with your local ethos and eroding the base of your mother tongue skills.

1.4 English Today—'Amalgamation of Influences'

> English is an amalgamation of several influences,
> Which goes to show that eliminating clashes
> Has been its mission, for ages.

As I mentioned earlier, the period of Modern English extends from the 16th century to this very day.

The British originally spread the language to all four corners of the world, and the process of migration in the last 30-40 years has brought back many new varieties to the English shores. Apart from this factor, the two most important reasons for so many influences occurring on the language are the Industrial Revolution and the Information Technology Age.

Modern English has many more new additions. The two main factors for this rise in words are the Industrial Revolution and the Information Technology wave, which have generated the need for new words. Due to constant upheavals in the modern era, and the subsequent rise and growth of the technological society, English's lexical bank is growing richer day by day.

English is a pluricentric language; this basically means that there is more than one version of Standard English, with American English and South British English being the main ones. There are several dialects and varieties spoken across the world as a result of the amalgamation of influences. There are distinct regional forms of the English language spoken in countries like New Zealand, Australia, Nigeria, Hong Kong, Canada, even in India and many other parts of the world. Even within Britain, there are distinct varieties—Irish, Scots and Welsh English. These varieties are similar to regional dialects that we all experience in our local regions, but there is one major difference—varieties of English affect entire regions or nations; they affect millions of people. Remember, there is nothing wrong or incorrect about these varieties, just that they are *different*. There are three main aspects to be kept in mind while dealing with these varieties:

(a) These varieties are all learned patterns of behavior.

(b) These varieties are all cultural products.

(c) A plethora of factors like background and education influence the creation and growth of these varieties.

These are some examples of the varieties of English:

American: She's gotten better.

Indian: The hockey coach is a real enthu guy.

Philippine Pidgin: hau kam?

British: I don't know where it is.

African American Vernacular English: I ain't trust you.

Slang: Okie dokie.

Dunglish: Put your cell phones out.

Manglish: Is that true ah?

Internet English: G2G. HAND. (In plain English, it means, Got to go. Have a nice day.)

As you can see from the examples, the varieties of English or New Englishes have their own cultivated, standard register. They facilitate the concept of code-switching, where people alternate between languages. Code-switching, in a way, preserves the local identity, which has an English dimension to it too thereby ensuring that each and every nation using English has a share in its ownership. It is like living two separate and parallel lives. In multilingual communities, the situation becomes a lot more complex as there are people relying on two or more languages thereby leading to the creation of more Englishes.

> **A Word of Caution**
>
> One may think that words like anchor or garden have the same meanings in both British and American English. In reality, it is not true; they are subtle differences in meaning when it comes to British English and American English.
>
> Several words like lift, minor and pass out have their respective meanings in British and American English, and also a meaning common to both British English and American English.
>
> One needs to be extremely careful while using words. One needs to use the words not only keeping in mind the context, but also paying attention to the kind of variety of English.
>
> Just knowing the meaning of the word is not enough; you also have to know its usage.

For people who do not have the resources to study English, the dialects of English is a blessing in disguise for them, as these local flavors help them to connect with their immediate world.

With the growing emergence of non-geographical economic affiliations, English will continue to influence other languages and cultures, and vice versa. This amalgamation is very crucial for exchanging not only linguistic aspects, but also sharing and borrowing from the cultural and spiritual spheres. This kind of borrowing and sharing definitely indicates absorbing a pantheon of popular words associated with these spheres. New words are being added at a breakneck speed from new concepts like the blogosphere.

Countries like Hungary have recognized the importance of these facts and influences, and hence have introduced English as a compulsory subject in primary education. It is sad to note that there are countries which want to promote English learning, but due to the lack of proper planning, government support, practical education policies and financial shortcomings, they are unable to realize the same.

A Word of Caution

One of the most significant characteristics of English is Orthography. Orthography is the study of correct spelling according to established usage.

Incorrect spellings can put you in embarrassing situations.

English has relatively complicated spelling rules. Therefore, you need to identify methods and tips that will suit your learning goals and help you to develop interest in words.

1.5 Comparison of Statistics—'Vis-à-vis Other Languages'

No language has had such a great magnitude
As English,
And this is what makes it so valued.

In more than 90 countries English has official or special status. With major trends like economic independence in terms of free trade and the open door policy, English more than any other language, has played a major role in forging economic alliances and providing administrative cohesiveness to several countries. Its supranational reach is unstoppable thereby providing thousands of opportunities for unique networking.

English is far more worldwide in its distribution than all other spoken languages. The relative importance of English as a foreign language can be further stressed with the fact that students tend to receive more instruction in English than they do in any subsequent languages they choose to study.

Young people in most developed nations prefer to embrace new words from English than from any other language. Non-native English speakers now outnumber native ones.

These are some interesting statistics related to this language, which you might be interested in knowing.

Table 1.1: Interesting Facts and Figures

Aspect	*Fact 1*	*Fact 2*
Geographic reach	Countries using English as either a first language or a second language are located on all five continents.	English is the most commonly studied foreign language in the European Union states.

(*Contd...*)

Aspect	*Fact 1*	*Fact 2*
The number of speakers and learners	Majority of the speakers belonging to international institutions, political bodies and the business community communicate in English.	English language teaching is a major growth industry. The revenue earned from English education-related exports is on the rise. English language learners are the fastest growing segment of the student population.
The volume of information, communication, knowledge stored and shared	Almost 75 per cent of the information on the Internet is in English. Most people use English to communicate using Short Message Service (SMS).	English speakers account for more than 40 per cent of the users on the Internet.
Special status, Official language, Foreign language	It is one of the six official languages of the United Nations (UN). The International Telecommunication Union (ITU) has six official languages and one of them is English.	More than 750 million people speak English as a foreign language.
Number of fields, areas	English is the gateway to global economic growth and technology transfer. English is the vehicle of a more advanced technology. Right from rescue workers to international banking, right from international tourism to Korean students, English reigns.	Several top research universities are located in English speaking countries like the United States. English is required in the fields of scientific publication, arts, diplomacy, international organizations, law, trade, music, medicine and the list goes on.

From the above table, it is clearly evident how important English is. In a world that is becoming more and more *flat*, mastering English gives a *competitive edge* over the others.

Till date, no other language has been able to match this growth. Why do you think English has become so popular? The reason is simple—English has always been the central theme of various revolutions, right from the British colonial period in the 17th and 18th centuries to the Industrial Revolution which began in the 18th century. Later on, in the late 19th century and early 20th century English once again found itself in the *right place* at the *right time* and doing the *right thing*. During this period, it was the central theme in the rise of America as a superpower.

The most indelible phenomenon of recent times is the Computer Revolution, which again has its roots in America. The computers were all programmed by Americans. There you go...the English influence was there yet again. The computer commands and instructions were all in English, rather what else they could be coded in. Press Ctrl+Alt+Tab to shutdown. Sounds familiar?

At regional levels, English may compete with German in Germany or with Hindi in India, but at the global level it is supreme.

1.6 Questions for Reflection

1. What important facets can you learn by studying the history of English?
2. What are the reasons for the exponential growth in demand for learning English?
3. What advantages have you had because of being bilingual/multilingual?
4. Will the emergence of English as a global language result in the disappearance of minority languages?
5. How do you perceive the growth and importance of the English language?

1.7 Chapter Recap

A. English, which began 1600 years ago as a means of communication in the British Isles, now makes its presence felt in every nook and corner of the world. We have literature from the Old English period (such as the poem The Dream of the Rood) which shows that this was a linguistically and intellectually rich culture with a highly expressive language.

B. English has been a given special place, in one way or the other, in almost all parts of the global landscape. It is no wonder that this language is always in the news.

C. One of the most critical components needed to prepare for the future is the power of information. In current times, people who possess this power are the ones who have good command of English.

D. English is the linguistic engine driving the wheels of globalization.

E. Today, English is listed as the official or co-official language of over 90 countries.

F. The two most important reasons for so many influences occurring on the language are the Industrial Revolution and the Information Technology Age.

G. The timeline of this language can be divided into three distinct phases: The Old English Period: 500-1100, The Middle English Period: 1100-1500 and The Modern English Period: 1500-Present.

H. There is a remarkable variety based on sounds, pedagogical norms, spellings, grammar and vocabulary within the English-speaking world.

I. People all over the world have realized the importance of English language acquisition.

J. English is a pluricentric language; this basically means that there is more than one version of Standard English, with American English and South British English being the main ones.

K. With the growing emergence of non-geographical economic affiliations, English will continue to exert its influence over other languages and cultures, and vice versa.

L. In a world that is becoming more and more *flat*, mastering fluency in English gives a *competitive edge* over the others.

What Sets the English Language Apart— 'So Many Aspects'

2

English is the *lingua franca* of the modern day
And it is here to stay.
Let us unlock the Global Growth Gateway;
It is English all the way!

Why has English become so popular? Is it the pronunciation? Is it the grammar? Is it the spelling? At the superficial level, these could be the reasons for its worldwide reach. But more than these structural factors of the language, it is its *inherent* quality of granting access to knowledge resources and enabling people to participate in world affairs which makes English so popular.

The first aspect that sets English apart is that it is spoken as the first or second language by more people in the world than any other language. McArthur states that English is the "universalizing language of the human race" (McArthur, 2002).

The importance of English is not only gauged by number of people speaking it, but also by the purposes for which it is used. It is used right from multinational companies to home computers. English as a language is an effective means of expressing ideas. This movement of ideas from one brain to the other through the vehicle of English is remarkable.

Apart from the main varieties of English like the American English, British English and Australian English, there are several local and regional varieties prevalent in places like Trinidad, Guyana and Belize to name a few.

> **Spotlight**
> It doesn't matter what the local variety of English is, no matter in which far flung part of the world it is spoken, all this goes to show that it is a 'Global Brand Ambassador'.
> English is everywhere, and in English, everybody is equal.

There are people who speak English, and then there are people who wish to speak English. Today, we see all these people researching brand new career avenues by breaking the traditional paths of progress. They want innovative alternatives and the best deals. They simply want more and this more is possible due to English.

2.1 Features of English—'The Perfect Blend'

High grades, an international job offer
Or excellent communication skills,
All this and much more, English promises to offer.

The main requirements to meet the needs of the modern world are:

(a) A well-structured and sophisticated education system.
(b) A culture of common values.
(c) An integrated knowledge base deriving value from several disciplines.
(d) A voice in world affairs.

And all of the above is possible and feasible due to English.

Do you want to:

(a) be able to communicate, negotiate, debate, convince with ease?
(b) bag an international job offer?
(c) earn excellent grades in an UK university?
(d) earn admiration and respect of classmates, co-workers?
(c) bc ablc to travcl abroad without difficulty?
(f) add new skills and technical knowledge?
(g) be able to converse well with native speakers of English?

All of this and much more is feasible with English in your skill set.

One language is never enough—for non-native linguaphiles, when it comes to learning additional languages, English is the first choice.

> **Spotlight**
>
> Imagine you are on an international flight to your business destination. You are carrying a world-class business magazine (the magazine is in English) with you and you decide to read it during the flight.
>
> As you start reading the magazine, the person seated next to you, looks at the magazine cover and then gives you a long look of admiration stashed with a hint of jealousy.
>
> Don't you feel satisfied to the core? Your time and investment in learning the English language has paid off really well.

Increasing command of this language is about ensuring that you make the 'right' impression. By being able to effectively communicate your views, thoughts and ideas to people, you can open up the door to unlimited opportunities.

Table 2.1: Features and Advantages of English

Sr. No.	*Features*	*Advantages*
1.	Versatility	Facilitates the sharing of educational experience, accommodates modern influences, yet retains the roots of the past, and when it comes to the international context, English is the only tongue capable of full expression.
2.	Global presence	Plays a major role in the political, economic, social and cultural aspects, and creates a culture of common values.
3.	Growth-driven	Provides upward social mobility and builds an integrated knowledge base.
4.	Learner-friendly	Connects people and provides motivation for learning.
5.	Rich vocabulary	Has great descriptive power and provides linguistic flexibility in terms of lexical alternatives.

2.1.1 Versatility—'Vivid, adaptable and expressive'

English is a vivid, adaptable, expressive and impressive language, and English earns high brownie points for itself for these features. It is a versatile language accommodating modern influences and constantly evolving with them, yet retaining a connection to its past. It is not merely about a particular region or a peculiar accent, but rather its main focus is on sharing educational experience and a wealth of literature and culture. The process of enablement through English learning, in a way, helps to bridge the gap between the 'haves' and the 'have nots'.

English has done away with the distinction between the formal and informal second-person modes of address. This aspect of English makes it apt for international interaction.

English is a crazily creative language, and that is why, when the stars are out, they are visible, but when the lights are out, they are invisible.

It is interesting to note that some people are inspired to learn English just because their favorite pop idols sing in English or their favorite stage artists are from the Queen's land. Isn't this versatile? Yes! And the reason is obvious. Every country has its own set of popular singers, singing in their own native language, but only a few manage to break into international limelight and this is possible only if they are humming in English. Another powerful impact of English as a means of expressing lyrics is that it acts as a unifying force, and these lyrics appeal to the youth especially, as they symbolize an icon of freedom, contemporary age and modern thought.

Inventions, professions, local customs and communication situations create new phrases and words. The *go-with-the-flow* quality of this language accommodates them all. Indeed, it is the first open source language.

English and its propensity to change and to be changed make it such a flexible tongue. It easily adapts to new features, when it comes in contact with the melting pot of local elements. And it is these different accents, social and cultural contexts that make English such a vivid and adaptable language. Over the years, English has become more and more contextualized to serve the needs of various people and communities across the globe. Based on context changes, English accommodates words from another language.

Each and every language meets the social and psychological needs of its speakers, but when it comes to the international context, English is the only tongue capable of full expression.

2.1.2 Global Reach—'From grassroots to global'

Whether you are living in the icy cold city of Norway or struggling to survive in the scorching heat of Mumbai, you are bound to encounter street signs, vendor shouts and local greetings in English. Due to its global reach, a strong non-native presence is developing at all levels. English has today become what Latin was to the world in the past.

However, English has not achieved its present status without a struggle. Within the last 40-50 years, there have been several attempts to establish artificial languages like Esperanto as the international means of communication. None of these attempts have made a favorable impression.

There has never been a time when so many people are sharing ideas and views across nations. There has never been a time when so many nations are communicating with each other. There has never been a time when so many companies are closing deals across boundaries. And never has there been a more urgent need for a global language. This global stature that English has achieved is more do with its rapid spread in the last 50 years than just with the total number of English speakers. Indeed, English is the medium for conveying all the nuances of human thought and action.

A cascade of advancements on the Internet frontier is causing interactive communities to spring up based on common aims and interests, and of course collaborating with each other through English. This new form of social interaction without boundaries is increasing the perimeter of English, even more.

Whether it is a global peace program or a political protest, you will find English as an integral part of the program/protest. The reason is loud and clear—English provides a vast perimeter thereby enabling your opinion/purpose/demand/message to reach out further to the world.

Quite often, a search for a regional place or local news on the Internet returns results with the following line attached to them 'content available in English'. The reverse scenario is a rare case.

English plays a major role in the political, economic, social and cultural aspects of the following countries:

Table 2.2: The Influence of English

Sr. No.	*Country Name*	*Sr. No.*	*Country Name*
1.	Antigua	2.	Australia
3.	Bahamas	4.	Barbados
5.	Belize	6.	Bermuda
7.	Botswana	8.	Brunei
9.	Cameroon	10.	Canada
11.	Dominica	12.	Fiji
13.	Gambia	14.	Ghana
15.	Grenada	16.	India
17.	Ireland	18.	Jamaica
19.	Kenya	20.	Liberia
21.	Malawi	22.	Malta
23.	Mauritius	24.	New Zealand
25.	Nigeria	26.	Pakistan
27.	Philippines	28.	Puerto Rico
29.	Senegal	30.	Seychelles
31.	Singapore	32.	South Africa
33.	Swaziland	34.	Tanzania
35.	Trinidad & Tobago	36.	Uganda
37.	United Kingdom	38.	United States of America
39.	Zambia	40.	Zimbabwe
41.	And many more....		

After World War II, English slowly and steadily began to extend its spread. And this was the beginning of an overall linguistic dominance, first in Europe and then globally, which indicates a continual rise in its volume and degree of frequency in international interactions.

Let me explain the global reach of English with an example. The power of English can take a business executive across countries in a smaller amount of time. Thanks to the aviation industry, and a greater thanks to English, which is why he is able to strike deals in so many countries. Early in the morning, he is in Jakarta where he closes a deal, and then he moves on to his next business halt. After stopping by in Singapore for a short interval of time to collect some important papers, he again takes to the high skies, and after a few hours the executive enters Tokyo to discuss the new deal with his Tokyo-based bosses. Several hours later, he reaches his native country United States, a place located far off on the other side of the planet. With the English language in your traveling kit, meeting people from different places in the world is greatly possible in this era of globalization.

English as an international language holds a dominant position even in countries where British colonization has had insignificant influence.

Knowledge is a process of enlightenment and empowerment. From the above points, we can witness for ourselves how English supports this process. This language is a store house of cultural, political, economic, social and historical wisdom.

Even independent and advanced nations like Germany and Switzerland endorse the usage of English. In countries like Iraq, where Arabic and Kurdish are the official languages, stupendous efforts are being made to include English too.

You ask a friend, a colleague or a relative "who is your favorite actor/pop singer/politician/author?" and you will get a name of a performer who has attained global recognition. Why so? The reason is simple—a huge number of celebrities are those who have attained global recognition because they are English speaking, and hence perform/sing/campaign/write in English. That is the kind of power English can give anyone—to rise from the depths of struggle to the heights of glory.

2.1.3 Spontaneous Conversation—'Break the ice'

Although the colonial days are long over, the Queen's language still remains potentially a strong communicative medium. A strong base in English can aid you to use the language to express contemporary real life situations.

A combination of quality reading, listening fluency and communication with native speakers, and of course, laced with the right idioms and quirks of speech, helps you to strike spontaneous conversations. That is the beauty of English. This in turn leads to community building as people learn to relate to one another's needs in a much more connected way. One needs to relate to the global richness of this language in the wider communication context in order to be able to create not only great conversations, but also enable higher-order thinking.

Using English for striking conversations has a dual advantage. Firstly, spontaneous conversations facilitate constant learning of new phrases, terms and experiences. Secondly, apart from the linguistic gains, the involved individuals learn to establish a sense of identity through this language as they learn to negotiate meaning and use it according to the context. This in turn helps to develop a broader-level perspective towards others and their viewpoints. One of the main ways of capitalizing on this feature of English is to apply classroom lessons in the real world. Move beyond the classroom curriculum!

In this global world, our actions have a global impact. For this reason, it is essential that we engage in collective multi-participant actions to share and connect diverse experiences. To address and solve the many issues faced by us and to protect the integrity of cultures in a hybrid world, we need to strike spontaneous dialogs in order to bring to the table, solutions, experiences, views and ideas of the millions of minds.

Flawless conversation in English promises, among other things, upward social mobility and intercultural competencies, and this is what attracts people the most.

Imagine the benefits you would accrue from sophisticated mannerisms that have the icing of English! (Thinking out loud.)

2.1.4 Easy to Learn—'Only if you are persistent'

Due to its learner-friendly structure, speakers of English can express the contextual and emotional meaning in clear and crisp terms. It helps to exchange ideas from one person to another, concisely and more accurately than any other language. Now with Internet-driven learning tools, resources and information for mastering this language are everywhere, not just in textbooks.

No language is easy or hard, but what makes it practicable, is a strong desire to learn. A strong motivation level is what is required to learn English. (The same principle applies to learning any other language.) When this instinctive motivation to learn this language comes as naturally to a learner as leaves to the branches, then the learner is bound to become an autonomous performer.

The need for international acceptance is something which drives people to learn English, and this is the reason that fuels their passion for learning. This passion, in a way, makes the language look and sound easy. This quality of English acts as a motivator to new learners of the language.

In one of my trips to Rome, Italy, I got a chance to visit a small village, where I interacted with some old folks. Through my conversation, I posed questions to them regarding the English language and one of the questions I asked them was "What is your take on learning the English language at your age?" The answers to this question brought out an interesting viewpoint. Most of them said, we are too old to learn it that easily, but we definitely want our children and grandchildren to learn it. They will find it easy to grasp as they are still very young and have a highly receptive mind.

Important observation: Age and profession are important factors in determining the motivation level for learning English. If you are a grandmother in your seventies, your inclination towards English might be minimal. But if you are an entrepreneur in Malaysia, you will desire to learn English by choice.

Spotlight

In one of my trips to Manila, I was surprised to hear a local vendor speak fluent conversational English. From the expressions on my face, he could make out what I was thinking, and he reacted by saying: "Whether you are at a taxi stand or in a post office or opening a bank account, you need to be able to speak in English, both fluently and with confidence".

I have a lot of respect for any person who learns a second language. It shows that they have fervent enthusiasm to enhance their wisdom in order to achieve their goals.

2.1.5 Rich in Vocabulary—'The more the merrier'

The vocabulary of English is undoubtedly vast. Present-day English has absorbed material from many other tongues. Dozens of new forms of English have already been spawned around the world. There is no other language which has more synonyms than English. It is said that if a word is used in English, it is acceptable universally.

English is continuously assimilating foreign words, causing English to have a larger vocabulary than any other language in the world. This assimilation has grown exponentially in the modern era. Languages that have influenced English include French, Latin, Greek, Dutch, Portuguese, Sanskrit, Hindi, German, Italian, Malay and many more.

As English has a plethora of words in its word bank, it provides the greatest descriptive power. This width of vocabulary helps speakers all around the world to describe the most complex of meanings in an expressive way. Thus, it makes sense to enrich your own word bank by adding rich English words on a day-to-day basis. The Global Language Monitor, a company that documents, analyzes and tracks trends in language usage, announced that the English language had crossed the 1,000,000 word threshold on June 10, 2009. Even the *Oxford English Dictionary* lists about 500,000 words and an additional half-million scientific and technical terms remain uncatalogued.

Enriching our vocabulary has become a lot easier. New words are at our fingertips, through the medium of mobile phones and keyboards.

A Word of Caution

English, a verbal treasure chest, needs to be used with caution. There are several words which have similar meanings (but it does not mean they have the exact same meaning), and these near-synonyms cannot be used as substitutes for each other. They need to be used in conjunction with the context.

For example, decline and reduce have a similar meaning, but with reference to somebody's failing health, we use decline and not reduce.

A person who is a computer master brain is definitely admired for his technical knowledge and subject matter expertise. But what is the point if he is not able to share and explain his views, theories and discoveries in clear and precise terms, just because he lacks the knowledge of the correct vocabulary. His reputation goes down! Speaking with a poor vocabulary can cause people to look down on you. Hence, regular conversation drills are important in English speaking. Mere knowledge is not enough for surviving the shockwaves of today's competition. The right tool—English is needed to implement, share and build upon the knowledge base.

Spotlight

In addition to your curriculum vitae, technical skills and appearance, what also matters is your English vocabulary. People not only judge you by your appearance, but also by your linguistic jugglery.

Virtually every language in the world has contributed to the development of English. Due to loan words from so many languages, English is popular for its lexical alternatives. The multiple identities of English operating in various cross-cultural contexts and the accommodative nature of this language give it a 'cosmopolitan feel', which is yet another reason for its global status. Linguistic heritage and values of almost all nations are integrated into English through these loan words.

English represents the several changing voices, which keep on increasing from generation to generation. Changing voices imply changes in the language as a result of economic, social, cultural and political factors. With new tools, inventions and products in several industries, derivation of new words, phrases and expressions is bound to occur. In non-native English speaking nations, food items, lifestyle-related terms, religious practices, customs and other social/ethnic factors lead to new lexical creations and add fresh dimensions to this language. These aspects make this language *internationally* appealing.

2.2 Lesson 1—'Right Words, Right Order, Right Time, Right Place'

Illustration 2.1: Do Not Mess up the Word Order

Messing up the order of words not only projects a poor image of the speaker, but also leads to confusion, misinterpretation and sometimes even a shock. As shown in this illustration, due to the incorrectly worded message from the old lady, the old man is in an utter state of confusion. He is completely lost as he does not know who Lawn is.

Mourning is way too far off from mowing, and a word which we all do not like at all. The right combination can create magic. Choosing the right words, in the right order, at the right time, and in the right place, needs both carefulness and creativity. Only then communicative success will follow.

A Word of Caution

Context matters—Use the right words, in the right order, in the right place, and at the right time. Know the difference between related words and phrases. For example, travel, trip, sojourn, journey, all these words have the same meaning, but they need to be used wisely, according to the context.

I sojourned to London by air...may sound correct to the ears, but technically speaking, I traveled to London by air is perfect.

2.3 Advice on Going Abroad to Learn English—'Diversify Your Learning Aids'

Do not be intimidated by the English language,
Instead leverage its power
To diversify your knowledge.

Learning a language is about learning to understand the world from the point of view of another culture.

In our ever-shrinking world and in the on-going internationalization of societies, *going global* is the key to having worldwide experiences. English is one of the most effective means of becoming a global citizen.

The first question that you need to ask yourself "Is studying English abroad something you are really interested in?" If you are armed with a positive mindset, then a foreign trip or an immersion camp is the best way to study the English language. As the language is everywhere, you really cannot get away from it. Studying this language in its natural settings results in deriving the right meanings from the context and using the perfect cadences.

If you are looking for a quasi-vacation, then short exchange programs or a one-semester course is a great option to learn this language.

The biggest hurdle that paralyzes learners is not about how to speak, how to write or how to read this language, but it is how to organize their learning habits and patterns to assimilate the English-speaking culture, it is about thinking about *thinking* in English.

Hundreds of people leave the comforts of their homes to master this language in countries like United Kingdom, Australia and United States, but only few are able to realize their dream. The reason is simple—PRACTICE. Learning any language requires practice—lots of practice! In other words, learning English should be ingrained in you as a good habit and which you should follow religiously.

A month long practice of positive self-talk is a sure-fire way of overcoming all language barriers. Positive affirmations like "my English is getting better and better" or "I am doing really well", help you to maintain a laser-sharp focus on your aims. Positive statements like these, act as a constant motivating factor in the entire learning life cycle.

Before setting out, do make it a point to learn about the history of English in context of the country you are visiting. Familiarize yourself with the culture and language nuances in order to adjust well with them.

Another very important factor that needs to be researched thoroughly, before embarking on your learning program, is what options and methods are available for practicing this language. Apart from the methods and tools available in the classroom environment, it is imperative to have access to this language in terms of reading, speaking and listening even outside the formal educational setting. The 'outside' environment could be your part-time job or even your hostel canteen. In other words, there needs to be a constant flow of fresh content, which takes your English to the next level.

Different countries have different education systems, and to choose the best system for yourself, you need to study the pros and cons of these systems. Opt for programs that emphasize results, not just inputs.

Apart from the length, quality and type of course or degree, what also needs to be considered is the cost factor.

You need to constantly be bombarded with English 'inputs'. To improve your speaking skills, you need to listen more and to improve your writing skills, you need to read more. This in a way prepares you to be ready for a complex and multicultural global economy.

2.4 Self-Survey of English Worksheet

The Self-survey of English worksheet helps one to gauge one's proficiency level in English. Answer the following questions and you yourself will know where you stand in regards to your level of comfort with the English language.

1. What kind of advantages do you experience in your profession due to your knowledge in English?
2. Are there any areas in this language that you need to improve upon?
3. What kind of books/genres do you like to read in English:
   (a) Biography
   (b) Fantasy
   (c) Memoirs
   (d) Short stories
   (e) Science fiction
   (f) Any other genre
4. Which international business magazines/journals do you read in English and on a regular basis?
5. To what extent these business magazines/journals help you in your daily life?
6. Rate yourself on a scale of 1 to 5 (1 being least proficient and 5 being highly proficient) for the following factors:
   (a) Understanding the context of the situation and reacting appropriately.
   (b) Understanding implied meaning conveyed by others.
   (c) Paraphrasing what others say without distorting the original meaning.
7. How often do you (1-Never, 2-At times, 3-Always)
   (a) omit the articles a, an and the.

(Contd...)

(b) get confused between the usage of adverbs and pronouns (someone, no one, everywhere).
(c) fail at understanding metaphors and figurative language.

8. How often do you use slang words like kidding, fab, all this, thing, stuff, etc., in your sentences?
9. Which language do you use most frequently at home? If not English, then how much percentage of time do you devote to its usage at home?
10. What is your favorite media? How much time do you spend with it each day?
11. Rate yourself on the following factors (Advanced, Average, Beginner, Low Proficiency, No Proficiency):
    (a) Speaking skills
    (b) Comprehension skills
    (c) Listening skills
    (d) Reading skills
    (e) Writing skills

Rate the following statements (Ratings—1: Always True, 2: Mostly True, 3: Sometimes True, 4: Mostly False, and 5: Always False.)

1. Do you refer to dictionaries for new words?
2. Are you able to grasp the gist of the content from the headlines/key words?
3. Are you able to grasp the message by studying the illustrations, tables and figures?
4. Do you get anxious whenever you have to appear for a reading comprehension test?
5. Do you exhibit the ability to use appropriate phrases to enrich the meaning of your message?
6. Do you identify and use parts of speech correctly (dependent clauses, subjects, verbs)?
7. Do you have any reading strategies for improving your reading comprehension? If yes, then how often do you revamp them?

2.5 Local Version—'International Flavors'

The underlined words in the following sentences are some of the words that we use in the localized version of English. What is the English counterpart for each of the underlined words?

(a) She likes shopping in the city bazaar.

(b) My mother won a crore in the state sweepstake contest.

(c) We must perform each and every dharma with all sincerity.

(d) His father is my guru.

(e) He loves to have chocolate cookies with a hot cup of chai.

2.6 Questions for Reflection

1. Do you think due to the global reach of the English language, linguistic diversity is being sacrificed?
2. Why improving vocabulary is necessary?
3. Which of your goals do you think English will help you to fulfill?
4. What makes English as a suitable universal language?
5. How many hours per week do you devote for improving English?

2.7 Chapter Recap

A. The inherent quality of granting access to knowledge resources and enabling people to participate in world affairs is what makes English so popular.

B. It doesn't matter what the local variety of English is, no matter in which far flung part of the world it is spoken, all this goes to show that English is a 'Global Brand Ambassador'.

C. One language is never enough—for non-native linguaphiles, when it comes to learning additional languages, English is the first choice.

D. Increasing command of this language is about ensuring that you make the 'right' impression. By being able to effectively communicate your views, thoughts and ideas to people, you can open up the door to unlimited opportunities.

E. Versatility, global reach, spontaneous conversation, easy to learn and rich in vocabulary, is what makes English such a feature-rich tongue.

F. The accommodative nature of this language gives it a 'cosmopolitan feel', which is yet another reason for its global status.

G. Virtually every language in the world has contributed to the development of English. Due to loan words from so many languages, English is popular for its lexical alternatives.

H. Messing up the order of words not only projects a poor image of the speaker/communicator, but also leads to confusion, misinterpretation and sometimes even a shock.

I. Studying the English language in its natural settings results in deriving the right meanings from the context and using the perfect cadences.

J. Many aspects like motivating factors, course, duration, cost, etc., need to be properly researched before embarking on your English learning program.

3 Role of English in Economic Modernization—'The Route to Sustainable Growth'

To tune into the rapidly changing marketplace,
English needs to have a central place
In the corporate agenda.

There is no doubt that we are living in times of great economic changes. The present age is pre-eminently an age of economic progress. English is more than just a communication tool; it is the motor which adds momentum to this economic progress. It facilitates the development of professional communities and networks. English opens new perspectives on life, enriches the cognitive background and broadens our minds. The role of economic modernization is an important one as it helps in maintaining financial stability and economic equilibrium, and English is the factor that helps nations to achieve both these factors so that they can be recognized as a strong and stable global entity.

English represents a vast reservoir of knowledge, and in current times, knowledge is one of the key factors in facing the stiff competition. In other words, English is the gateway which grants access to one and all to the ocean of knowledge in fields of technology, research, politics and many more.

As more countries are becoming dollarized, English is crucial not only for the individual growth and excellence of professionals, but it is equally necessary for the smooth functioning of business entities. Any communication gap in terms of low/no competency in English translates to loss of goodwill and customer trust, loss of profitable deals, and overall tendency to fall behind in the race.

Developing countries need external communications to expand into the overseas market, and for doing so, English is the only vehicle of communication with the countries of the world.

The need for a common language is highly appreciated by the international business community. The technology-driven business world feels that it is easier to strike deals using one language, rather than spending time and money using translation/ interpretation services. Moreover, due to the technology explosion, business professionals have become more mobile and accessible, both physically and electronically. This growth in technology and the proverbial global village is possible not only due to latest gadgetry and tools, but it is also important to note that all these innovations are driven by one common language—English.

The exponential growth in international deals and multinational ventures would have not been possible, if only a few nations were a part of the global village. With practically the entire world logging into the global village domain, there has never been a time, when so many nations are talking to each other round the clock. These joint ventures involve a huge set of legal documents and agreements, which are mostly in English. This again gives rise to the demand for English specialists in this area.

On a global level, it has been observed through various surveys and studies that nearly 80 per cent of the business population uses English on a weekly basis and more than 50 per cent uses it on a daily basis. Another interesting aspect inferred from such surveys and studies is that 95 per cent of the organizations firmly believe that proficiency in English will improve the productivity of their employees.

As any academic year comes to an end, what takes the spotlight, are buzzwords like international exposure, a great job offer and 100 per cent placements. To convert these dreamy words into reality, what is needed, is the English language.

Excuses like "My English teacher in school is the main reason for my poor English skills" or "I am not so good at learning languages" will not work in today's world. Respect for, sensitivity towards and knowledge of this language is essential when you are operating on a worldwide scale. The expansion of the international business domain is slowly and steadily shifting the focus from English for academic purposes to English for more specialized purposes in order to cater to the 'real world' diverse needs of the working community. This shift is really helpful for professionals to succeed in their respective fields.

Nations which are majorly dependent on foreign investment need to lean onto the shoulders of English, so that they can leverage the power of English to cut down on the dependency level, and connect with the world and establish linkages with the world economy. The power of English is not only limited to monetary resources, but it also helps countries to build their soft power, which can bring about *incalculable* gains in the long run.

3.1 Importance of English in the Business World Survey

Regular revamps in English learning
Is the key to big earnings.

I interviewed 15 senior managers from various industries—IT, manufacturing, retail and finance. All these managers are high-end native speakers of English. The one question that I asked each one of them was "What happens when you receive a new concept proposal, a business plan or a report in English from a junior who is not good at the language?" And everyone echoed: "Lots of rework, redrafting and several rounds of revision". One of the respondents went on to say: "English is a powerful tool, which can bring us closer to the rest of the world".

Conclusion: Enterprises need to regularly revisit and revise with prudence their in-house, high-quality English training programs and also be ready to invest in hiring external English language trainers in order to bring their employees up to the mark. A combination of English language skills and business skills keeps you ahead in the race. English skills help to restructure company policies in real-time, keeping in line with the ever-changing business dynamics.

In order to be a dominant player in economic modernization, companies and individuals alike, need to demonstrate the following traits (of course, with the English touch to them)—

- Communicate with cogency
- Acknowledge and adapt to the challenges of the current times
- Think clearly
- Improve team-building skills
- Ask questions which invite constructive inputs
- Write in lucid terms
- Connect with international clients
- Appreciate views and events objectively

Apart from the above traits, what keeps one going is *continuous learning*, and English is your partner in this process.

Organizations want their employees to be great negotiators in increasingly team-oriented, metropolitan, intercultural workplaces. More and more companies are making considerable investment in ensuring that their workforce is competent in English. And with well-planned learning systems in place, employees too, are showing greater readiness to engage in language learning. This affirms the fact that English is one of the most vital elements of the workplace essential skills. This skill gives the employees the confidence to explore the opportunities and dissipate the challenges in the workplace.

Successful Communication = Successful Business Ventures

3.2 Economics and Demographics—'Results Say It All'

Being literate gives us advantages,
But being literate in English
Gives us advantages, galore.

Why discuss economics and demographics in relation to English? The reason is simple. Of the million or so business transactions that materialize around the world in any given day,

English dominates the scene. The technological tools and processes used to execute these transactions require an understanding of the language that drives this technology, which is *English*.

Transactions and operations in any field are English-driven. Whether it is services or the research field, whether it is generating comprehensive reports or preparing cutting-edge, commanding presentations, English is the focal point.

Currently, more than the actual monetary resources or GDP, what make a country successful are its economic differentiators in the form of knowledge, communication and innovation. All these three differentiators require action-centric skills, which only one language can nurture—English.

In present-day, decisions need to be taken in real-time for achieving the goals of international repositioning, cost cutting and economic diversification, and for this to happen English is needed. This is one of the main reasons for the fast growth of the newly industrialized countries.

The best jobs with an up-market feel to them go to those who can speak English. Especially, with foreign direct investment in the services sector, there is going to be a boom in the job market. To prepare for such a boom and to enhance employment opportunities, we need a combination of government supported English education system and policies, and efforts put in by other organizations like NGOs, private institutions and social bodies.

Spotlight

Mastery of English is mandatory for any professional working in the global business space.

No matter what efforts your organization is making to teach you Business English, you as an individual must invest efforts for honing your Business English skills.

I conducted an observation survey of 50 employees working for an international manufacturing firm. The observation period was of six months, which was used to keep track of their attitudes towards the English language, both before and after the English training program. The firm had invested a huge amount in imparting skills in English language to their employees. I constantly monitored their attitudes throughout the period of observation. There was a drastic change in their attitudes after the completion of the English training program. It was found that over the six months time frame, the number of respondents who said English was highly essential for growth in the workplace increased from 25 per cent to 90 per cent. Several factors are related to this growth. The pie chart indicates the percentage value for each of the factors, which the employees felt are achievable only with the power of English.

(a) Upward Mobility—40 per cent
(b) Career Development—29.2 per cent
(c) Better Pay—14.8 per cent
(d) New Skills—11.7 per cent
(e) Others (travel abroad, better lifestyle)—4.3 per cent

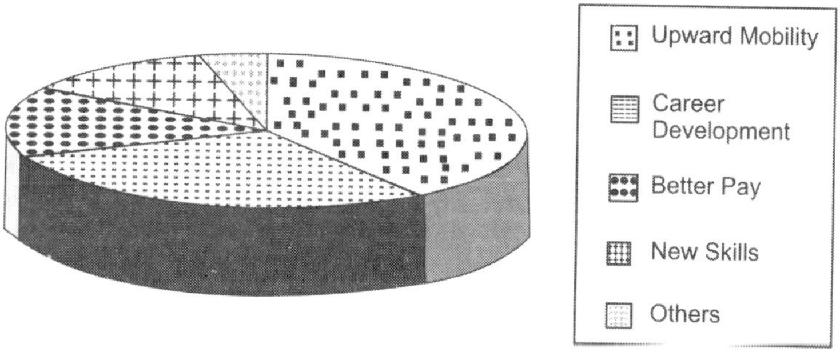

Figure 3.1: Growth and English Go Hand-in-Hand

3.3 Various Industries—'Listen, Speak, Write, Think and Deal in English'

Personnel qualified in English
Are considered as a valuable asset,
With which all losses organizations can banish.

Do you want to initiate contact with your international prospects in order to tap international markets? The only way to attract foreign clients to your products and services is by understanding their culture, of course, through the medium of English communication.

The survival and progress of any industry today hinges on its adaptability level to quick business changes. English is one such parameter that helps industries to face these changes successfully, which in turn helps these industries to grow their market share and make more international sales.

Do you want to take big leaps in your current job, by surpassing others and leaving them way behind? I am certain the answer is a universal YES. Underscoring the importance of education, the US Ambassador to India, Timothy Roemer said, "English is a global language and is connected to job opportunities".

With the advent of the global era, having a second or even a third language on your curriculum vitae is very beneficial. Organizations are bound to look at you as a 'valuable asset'. Especially in careers where clients may be anywhere on the globe, the ability to communicate with them in their own business language (which most of the times is English) results in business gains.

Even in India, the official language of the corporate world is English. Fluency in this language, on the résumé as well as in the practical mode, helps you to make phenomenal strides in the corporate world.

It is quite possible that your head is a dynamic powerhouse of business proposals, but you are not able to express them effectively due to the lack of proficiency in English. This may hamper your professional growth. English is the key to economic survival.

As English is the language of the Internet, it is but natural that players of the corporate game need to have a firm grasp of English in order to leverage the vast amount of business information available on the Internet.

A Word of Caution

In the case of personnel who possess poor English skills, a lot of hidden costs are involved like duplication of effort, loss of goodwill, delayed deliverables, and low employee morale.

English is a key factor in bridging barriers in business communication. Proficient speakers of English as a second language can be found here, there and everywhere.

The following aims can be achieved with competence in English and these are applicable across the wide spectrum of occupation sectors:

- Handle situations and people effectively
- Produce culture specific communication content
- Display professional conduct
- Usage of relevant phrases and terminology
- Perform international market research
- Show the ability to exceed the expectations of the customers
- Increase international sales
- Discover new business areas

The role of English in all the industries is not merely pertinent to economic growth or expansion of trade, but also helps to build and project the social and cultural identity of nations through its usage in several industries. This not only ensures better business, but also has a deep influence on the mindset of the customer chain.

3.3.1 Banking—'Bank on English'

The early 19th century had seen the rapid growth of the international banking system. This rapid growth proved to be a boon for international business ventures and investment opportunities. Today, the banking sector plays an instrumental role in the commercial economic activity, and at the same time facilitates consumer-related financial transactions. Money being a central factor in our lives, and banks being the main instrument for handling this factor, they need to be as open and transparent as possible in their operations.

English is a means of achieving a firm threshold in the market place, and this financial literacy is not only important from the banking staff's standpoint, but also equally important from the customer's end. One needs to be vigilant and savvy enough, to not fall into monetary scams spinning across the banking network.

Documents and statutes related to international regulations and banking laws are in English. It is imperative to be good at this language in order to prevent scams and track down fraudsters.

Apart from the domain knowledge, any banking professional also needs to upgrade his know-how about the various financial news, international trade and commerce regulations, accounting principles and latest statutes. These various aspects are connected with a gamut of banking-related professionals—accountants, corporate lending staff, auditors, economists, managers and the like. This sector is growing rapidly and to keep pace with this growth, one needs the knowledge of English in order to contribute as an international player in the economic space.

3.3.2 Publishing—'Publish in English and get noticed'

Just as in other fields like media or science, people who have a command of English have better chances of success and recognition, the same holds good for people associated with the publishing industry.

Today, major publishing conglomerates or independent publishing houses have to strike a balance between literary merit and commercial considerations. And they find it easier to strike this balance in English-driven literature. I surveyed a few of the top publishing houses and found out that 75 per cent of their titles are in English and the remaining in other languages. Another interesting finding that I dug up was that English titles are found in all genres (fantasy, self-help, cultural studies, etc.) and all publishing categories (academic, professional, management, etc.), whereas non-English titles are found in only certain genres and categories.

The publishing industry has really stepped up the pace in the last few years. This industry too comes out with comprehensive, need-based material. Several popular journals, newspapers and magazines have tie-ups with major publishing houses to launch up-to-date books in all genres, accompanied with electronic material. And all this happens in English, *majorly*. These factors generate more intellectual property in English.

Just as the starting point of the publishing cycle is crucial, so is the end point—marketing of the books. These days, due to the power and reach of the Internet, this industry just like any other industry wants to acquire more customers. A high percentage of the reader population is either English-speaking or interested in English books. Hence, publishing houses set aside a considerable amount of funds for gearing sales towards mass-market books, and all the publicity is done in English, of course.

The combination of just-in-time publishing options and English is definitely re-contouring the publishing landscape, and this is definitely making sure that the ultimate goals of mass production and mass consumption are being met.

So many popular books from non-native speakers have been translated into the ultimate language—English, this allows for global readership of a vast repertoire of culture and knowledge.

A Word of Caution

Since English is the predominant language in the publishing industry, authors writing in English have a much better chance of translation than those writing in other tongues.

Scholars in fields like humanities and medical researchers who want to share their papers and findings through books also resort to publishing their works in English.

3.3.3 Call Centers—'Value of customer service'

Do non-English speakers have a chance in the call center space? Call centers are also a growing business across the globe and anything to do with 'across the globe' has English as its *sine qua non*. No matter how huge or small a call center is, communication is the hub of all the activity. Better communication using English equates to more opportunities and tapping niche areas. English language helps to tap the global market and earn more clients. English occupies an important place in the call center training programs, be it in the sales department or the customer service department.

These days, most multinational service industries have either outsourced their work or established call centers in various countries. The survival of such service-oriented industry depends upon the kind of communication their representatives have with their customers. Comprehension of English is the stabilizing factor for striking a balance between cost and services provided, and in turn creating happy and loyal customers in the count of millions.

Communication in call centers is not about eloquence or articulation. Here the right attitude is the real figure of speech, which draws customers to your business. As the call center employees are dealing with worldwide customers, attention to detail is a must. Apart from crisp written skills, they need to pay attention to their pronunciation, nuances, word usage and grammar. Finally, any organization's image and market position is dependent on the performance of its employees. And English plays a major role in sustaining this image and goodwill amongst customers. One grammatical error or incorrect word acts as a repellant and sends the customers away to your competitors.

> **A Word of Caution**
>
> How different is different than from different from?
>
> Different than is used most of the time "Our product is different than...."
>
> Different from is used rarely, but it is the right usage.
>
> See the difference!

Call centers are point of systems; hence the message containing the information needs to be properly worded. An improperly worded message reflects a poor image of the company. Performance in call centers is all about grasping and comprehending English 'for the ear'.

In India, with the advent of globalization and the open-door policy, more and more international companies are opening up call centers. With a large population of educated English-speaking resources, the sky is the limit.

Learning English to do well as a call center officer/customer service representative does not entail merely speaking well, it also deals with many complex aspects. A fresher has to undergo intense training to master the following aspects:

- Call center phraseology
- Politeness training
- Speech clarity
- Cultural sensitivity
- Accent neutralization
- Listening
- Comprehension
- Telephone manners
- Recognize and respond to language varieties and dialects

All these factors are essential to correctly recognize situational communication requirements and service international callers accordingly. All the above aspects mean a lot of time and investment, but it is worth it all. As finally all these aspects map to great customer service and permanent customer relationship.

3.3.4 Aviation—'This is your pilot speaking'

Why do you think English is the main language of the aviation industry? Isn't this a rhetorical question? I am sure we all know the answer. During the rise of this sector in the 60s and 70s, UK and USA were the dominant players in the air game, and hence this dominance spearheaded the spread of this language over the high skies. The demand of English aviation is surely on the rise because of the rise in international air traffic, and now more nations are airborne than ever.

Obviously even with this single platform for aviation communication, a standardized version of the language is needed to avoid confusion and communication errors. This is where 'Airspeak' comes into play, a minimized version of English. 'Roger', 'Alfa', 'Charlie', do these code names ring a bell in your head? These are all aviation terms; a part of the controlled language used in aviation communication.

The lack of knowledge of English can lead to major accidents and eventually loss of life and destruction of property. In order to execute the necessary instructions accurately, to ensure that safety hazards precautions are in place and directions are correctly followed, the pilots, air traffic controllers and all the related staff need to be well-versed in English.

One of the worst plane accidents in the aviation history is the fatal collision of a Dutch KLM 747 into a Pan Am 747 in 1977, which was caused by miscommunication. The official report stated that "inadequate language" was the reason for this disaster. The Dutch pilot used the phrase "we are now at take-off", whereas he actually meant to say that he was now taking off. The air traffic controller misinterpreted it as "waiting on the runaway". We also need to understand that not all airborne accidents are due to a lack of linguistic skills. There are several other factors, both technical and non-technical, which can cause mishaps too.

Aviation English is not about daily routine communications. It involves a lot of technical terms, safety procedures, rules and regulations. Aviation-related personnel have to be very careful while communicating messages, especially in emergency situations. They have to be fully trained in presenting the required information in the most unambiguous and precise terms. The lack of skills in English is a big safety-related issue.

The International Civil Aviation Organization (ICAO) mandates a certain level of competency in English, determined by the Test of English for Aviation (TEA). Aviation phraseology is not only important for pilots, air traffic controllers, aviation companies and insurance companies, but also important for the passengers. As finally, it is the safety and comfort of the passengers that keeps any airline company going, or should we say 'flying high skies'.

The world is a rolodex of people and English provides an effective way of standardized standard operating procedures for handling this rolodex of people, which in turn facilitates safe aircraft operations internationally.

3.4 Business English—'A Clear-cut Edge'

Right from board room presentations
To high-end negotiations,
Business English helps
To strike lucrative bargains.

Business communication is the heart and soul of all the organizations, and what keeps this heart and soul in a performance-driven mode is English. A watered down understanding of the business terminology gets you nowhere. A thorough understanding of Business English is imperative. The global nature of the world economy implies that people from all corners of the globe must be able to communicate to do business with each other, and because English dominates the global scene, English for business purposes is bound to be widely used too.

Business English is way advanced than asking directions to the nearest bus stop. It is all about being professional and highly competent to be able to design cross-cultural solutions to meet global business demands. Business English is unlike the English that you speak in the classroom. Business English is English in the 'real' world (a world where there is no room for mistakes). My suggestion: commit every possible mistake in the classroom 'safe' environment because this is one place where you are allowed to make mistakes and correct them too.

Almost all international business meets, trade conclaves and world conferences are conducted in English. Even for internal correspondence, the text types that professionals read and write (reports, e-mails, official documents, letters and memos) are in English.

Business English is the passport to growth, power, knowledge, wealth and influence. It is a medium not only for worldwide commerce; it has become increasingly essential for inter-state business too.

Most international business procedures and transactions, including reports, agreements, contracts and electronic correspondence are written in English. This wealth of information is being generated at an amazing rate, and professionals who are unable to tap into this onslaught of information will definitely affect the bottom line, *negatively*.

If you are a Mexican doing business with a Malaysian counterpart, it is more likely that the two of you discuss the business deal in English, only if both of you are well-educated in it. Just imagine having to strike a deal using a mediator who knows both the languages. In such a scenario, no one can be sure as to what kind of information got exchanged.

Business English lets organizations expand their geographic outreach. In current times, raw materials, labor and other goods needed to develop goods and services come from all over the world, it is imperative to have a common language of negotiating and dealing—*English*.

Research figures indicate a steady growth in the number of organizations hiring employees who possess bilingual skills. In my earlier book on team management—*Organizational Democracy: Collaborative Team Culture: Key to Corporate Growth*, I have discussed how the positive energy vibes in a team need to be identified, nurtured and shared, and one of the ways for doing so, is a smooth communication workflow. To build and maintain this network of communication, English plays a crucial role; it is the main node of connectivity.

A Word of Caution

Business English is not about teaching or learning business in English, but is about using English in the business world or in the professional context.

Once you realize the deeper importance of Business English, you will certainly:

- Establish international contacts
- Analyze and predict with accuracy
- Be an expert at the online aspects of business like Internet marketing
- Synthesize knowledge and concepts
- Make better decisions
- Identify the main ideas

The 'bar' for expertise in Business English is getting higher in this highly interconnected world, and there are three simple steps—the **PBP** formula to be able to deal with Business English, *effectively*.

Practise new business terms and phrases that you pick up over each working day, either in presentations or in meetings.

Be heard by others, especially by your trusted peers so that they can give you instant and frank feedback about your work.

Polish your learning inputs based on the feedback received from your colleagues, partners and seniors.

This PBP cycle of assimilating business terms is an ongoing one. Business English learners need to maintain laser-sharp focus on their energies to be able to make the most from effective language learning activities and monitor the growth of their vocabulary and language skills. Often learners/students of English perform role play activities to get a professional feel of the environment they will be in, once they step into the corporate world. For example, students of tourism can be asked to perform role play exercises, in which they take up real life roles to handle occupation-related issues, for example, the ticket booking counter scenario.

The most important fact of capitalizing on English is that of creating an environment of 'immersion'. Do not impose it on the workforce rather find creative ways of ensuring that they are continuously updating their proficiency levels. Let me give you one such example, where a mix of business and pleasure does wonders—The Game of Scrabble. Organize Scrabble sessions that focus on business terms only, and you will find yourself learning at a much faster pace.

The focus of any activity/program/training aimed at honing Business English is to help employees to:

- Develop skills of intellectual and interaction stimulation.
- Deliver practical business value.
- Be aware of the meaning of provisions, policies and clauses.

- Understand the business situation and employ the right communication skills accordingly.
- Understand business protocols.
- Develop intercultural competencies.
- Recognize and repair communication breakdowns.
- Think about old problems in new ways.

3.5 Lesson 2—'Business English is Your Future'

Illustration 3.1: Spoken Business English, A Definitive Must Have

Looking at an advertisement board for Spoken Business English Classes, our dear old friend remembers what one of his friends said in their youth days, "When I was a child, I thought the world only had three languages—English, Hinglish and my mother tongue". Thinking to himself, our dear old friend is very much happy that he had realized much earlier in life that there are several types of English and some of these are highly important for moving ahead in life—Business English is what got him to climb to the top of the ladder.

Business English is fast becoming the deal breaker in today's recruitment process and hiring decisions.

3.5.1 Advantages—'You name it and you get it'

Employers are more interested in hiring employees who are forward-thinking. One of the main characteristics of being a forward-thinker is expressing keen interest towards learning the English language.

Another main advantage of learning a foreign or second language is that your ability to learn new languages improves. So why not start with English itself? Look at it this way, DUAL advantage. Firstly, English opens the doors to your future and secondly, it hones your language learning skills.

Learning Business English is necessary to have an error-free correspondence. Even if there is an automated spell-check program and grammar-check facilities available in computers, it is always better to back them up with manual error checking. Contextual meaning can be corrected only with human intervention. Imagine with such a crisp grasp over the business terminology, you could be the apple of the eye for some, while the object of envy for others.

With the right terms in your business kit, your business e-mails are bound to be flawless. The knowledge of how to use the right words to express the business plan, proposal or presentation makes all the difference in getting the message across, *lucratively*. This in turn adds momentum to career progression.

Your superiors immediately consider you as more competent than your peers because of your English finesse. When you develop a solid understanding of advanced and modern business concepts, terms and models, your business partners will consider you as an advanced English speaker and they will be much more likely to do business with you for a longer period of time.

I casually asked some street vendors about their opinion on English and 90 per cent felt that if they were given a chance to learn English, this opportunity would certainly change their lives, *for the better.*

Business English provides broad-based participation, which in turn can help in tapping alternative sources of information and lead to increased dissemination of vital business facts and figures.

3.5.2 Tricks of the Trade—'Be an active learner'

To improve your Business English, you need to have a game plan in place. Whether you do it on your own or hire a professional to do it, ensure that the methods and content of teaching is not about patronizing the English language. It is about helping employees to put their business knowledge in clear and effective terms, using the right business vocabulary and profession-related terms.

Activities can be undertaken in the form of seminars, workshops and conferences for being in constant touch with Business terminology. On an individual level, one could also do a lot of mirror practice, which helps to monitor speed and tone, and also helps to develop the right kind of jaw, lip and tongue movements to get the right pronunciation.

There are several factors—intellectual, professional and practical, which can further be classified into generic and specific factors that help you in determining your exact motivating aspect for learning the English language. Thus, you need to have a clear idea of *why* you want to learn English, as this will help to keep you anchored to your language learning goals.

An integral aspect of providing good customer service is in knowing the 'right' way to communicate and employing the 'accepted' ways of communicating with clients/business partners/ suppliers/end-users.

Constant monitoring of your daily conversational habits is a must. Do not feel uncomfortable even when you are talking to a native English customer or a native English counterpart in another office branch.

While operating in a multinational environment, accent improvement is a crucial element of Business English communication. It is all about learning to switch between accents depending on the context. It is also about softening the accent in order to sound like a native English speaker.

Remember that body language transmits a lot of information. Facial expressions and the right gesticulations can come to your rescue in the case of verbal failures. Economy in word usage in business scenarios helps to get the correct messages across to the audience.

Try to recall and apply new learning to business situations on a day-to-day basis. Finally, your competency in Business English is how the world sees you, and how you market yourself and your company.

Spotlight

The bottom line is to be an 'ACTIVE' learner, always!

If you want to play the global game of business, then you need to be equipped with the English gear.

The English gear lets you:

Build products that turn out to be a real cash cow.

Become a tough negotiator.

Carve out a niche for yourself in the corporate world.

Become a part of the movers and shakers clan.

Clinch million-dollar deals.

Be in a win-win situation (most of the times).

3.5.3 Assessment of the Business English Level Worksheet

It gives you an overall picture of your adeptness in Business English. Ratings and observations for each of the domain areas of English proficiency will help to gauge an employee's skill level and revise improvement plans and programs accordingly.

Employee Name:

Manager's remarks:

Overall rating for the Business English competency in various domain areas: (ratings—1: Excellent, 2: Good, 3: Average, 4: Below Average and 5: Poor)

Business communication:

Speaking:

Writing:

Listening:

(Contd...)

Comprehension: Vocabulary and Grammar: Cultural skills: Business Networking: Negotiation and Contracts:				
Performance Indicator	Agree	Disagree	Any other observations	Remedial measures
Communication Skills				
Uses clear communication with peers in terms of comments, questions, information sharing and business updates				
Communicates with the appropriate content for the given context (e-mails, reports, conference calls, etc.)				
Contributes to meetings and discussions in an effective manner				
Asks clear questions during brainstorming sessions				
Listening Ability				
Listens to others with attention, both in formal and informal settings				
Paraphrases others using appropriate sentences				
Responds appropriately to what others say				
Speaking Proficiency				
Speaks clearly in an audible tone and at a pace which can be understood well by colleagues				
Uses the right phrases, correct grammar and business terms to convey the message.				
Modulates voice and uses intonation patterns to lay emphasis				

(Contd...)

Pronounces words accurately				
Writing Skills				
Delivers accurate written information to queries posed by peers				
Knows how to use all the elements of business writing—start, reference, main details, closing, etc.				
Conveys the main idea/ objective of a business proposal, plan and contract using the most appropriate business terminology				
Comprehension Skills				
Grasps the main idea of the discussion, presentation				
Pays attention to the implied meaning				
Synthesizes communicated material/text to reflect personal interpretations of the same in an effective way				
Summarizes messages in crisp and lucid terms.				

Further Analysis of Business English Skills: (Short response—Yes/No or Observations)

a. Learns from mistakes
b. Plans before communication
c. Proofreads the content
d. Refers to reference books, dictionary and thesaurus to confirm the integrity of the communication
e. Shows the zeal for improvement
f. Uses evaluation and mental imagery techniques for smooth communication

3.6 Questions for Reflection

1. How important is the proficient and proper use of English in the daily workflow in your job?

2. What do you do to practise Business English in cyberspace and face-to-face meetings?
3. What kind of business leverage one tends to lose if one is ill-equipped as far as English skills are concerned?
4. Why does someone use English rather than his/her local language?
5. How often do you use English to do your job?

3.7 Chapter Recap

A. The present age is pre-eminently an age of economic progress. English is more than just a mere communication tool; it is the motor which adds momentum to this economic progress.

B. When you strike deals using English, the opportunities are limitless.

C. The power of English is not only limited to monetary resources, but it also helps countries to build their soft power, which can bring about *incalculable* gains in the long run.

D. A combination of English language skills and business skills is what will keep you ahead in the race.

E. Of the million or so business transactions that materialize around the world in any given day, English dominates the scene. The technological tools and processes used to execute these transactions require an understanding of the language that drives this technology, which is *English*.

F. English is the main language of several industries—banking, publishing, call centers and aviation.

G. On a global level, it has been observed through various surveys and studies that nearly 80 per cent of the business population uses English on a weekly basis and more than 50 per cent uses it on a daily basis.

H. Business English is the passport to growth, power, knowledge, wealth and influence.

I. More and more companies are making considerable investment in ensuring that their workforce is competent in English.

J. Employers are more interested in hiring employees who are forward-thinking. One of the main characteristics of being a forward-thinker is expressing keen interest towards learning the English language.

K. The survival and progress of any industry today hinges on its adaptability level to quick business changes. English is one such parameter that helps industries to face these changes successfully.

L. Several workplace aims like professional conduct, effective handling of business situations and the like can be achieved with competence in English, and these are applicable across the wide spectrum of occupation sectors.

M. Sectors like banking, publishing, call centers and aviation are growing rapidly. To keep pace with this growth, one needs the knowledge of English in order to contribute as an international player in the economic space.

N. Business communication is the heart and soul of all the organizations, and what keeps this heart and soul in a performance-driven mode is English.

O. Business English is English in the 'real' world, a world where there is no room for mistakes. Business English lets organizations expand their geographic outreach.

P. The PBP formula helps to hone your skills in Business English.

Q. An integral aspect of providing good customer service is in knowing the 'right' way to communicate and employing the 'accepted' ways of communicating with clients/business partners/suppliers/end-users.

R. Your competency in Business English is how the world sees you, and how you market yourself and your company.

S. The bottom line is to be an 'ACTIVE' learner, always!

4 English as a World Language—'Embraces the Needs of Everyone'

English is the window to the world,
Through which our dreams unfold
Into reality.

The world is talking and sharing more. English is our 'Window to the World'—we live in an age of Information Technology. Through this window, we have several avenues at our disposal, which help to keep ourselves abreast of all the latest happenings in any part of the world. English is the reflection of the aspirations, endeavors, local history, and experiences of diverse cultures.

There are several things that you encounter in modern living, which help to convince you that English has become a 'global necessity'. It lets you maintain a healthy balance between your physical space and virtual lives.

The very fact that this language is not bound to any linguistic constraints goes to show its reach. It is an *aterritorial* living legend.

English as a world language can be seen in three ways:

A. Rapid spread across the globe as a second/foreign language.

B. The growing impact of English in the various areas of life and business.

C. The increase in local/regional flavors of English.

English is the leading language of a whole lot of industries; it boasts of a widespread portfolio—advertisements, scientific journals, literary reviews, books, peace processes, science, consumerism, technical reviews, periodicals, newspapers, aviation, conferences, social movements, technology, diplomacy, sport, music and the list goes on.

Almost 75 per cent of the online stored information is in English. More than 70 per cent of the world conferences in the fields of science and technology are conducted in English. It is a major medium of education too. It offers us treasures of knowledge in all social sciences like economics, sociology, history, political science and many more. Till date, no other language has been able to match this growth.

There are five main aspects that make English the 'World Language'. These are:

- The geographic spread of English
- The number of speakers, learners of this language
- The volume of information, knowledge produced and shared in this language
- Special status, Official language, Foreign language
- The number of fields, areas and domains

It is interesting to note that English speakers and nations which were once colonized by this language are not just passively absorbing the language; they are actively reshaping and remaking it.

The bottom line is if you want to learn English, use it *extensively* and *correctly*. This rule is universal to all languages.

4.1 Reasons for Emergence—'As a Global Language'

American pop culture,
British colonialism,
And its cosmopolitan nature
Is what makes English internationally popular.

Paradigm shifts, where a whole community or nation changes the way they do things, are fast becoming the norm rather than the exception. These changes are happening in all areas of life, including linguistic needs and languages, especially the way in which the entire world is using English for various purposes.

English has this wonderful knack of doing the right thing as per the given context, be it the colonization period or today's era of an increasingly shrinking world. It is always there to bridge the gaps in global consciousness with its spread and flexibility. It lets us look at the world as an integral part of us. The rise of multinational organizations and international bodies of common interests has cemented its position even more.

At no point in history has any language traveled so far and wide as English has. Today, English is not merely considered as an international language, but it also represents a totally new phenomenon in human history. We need to look at this phenomenon with a new perspective and not view it as a symbol of the colonial past, only then we can realize its uniqueness of preserving diversity by making each speaker who uses this language to feel at home within its fold.

Presently, the rate of urbanization is ever-increasing. This increase is causing more and more people to not only migrate to advanced nations, but also make a move from rural areas to the city within their own nations. Both these forms of people movement have led to further *Englishification*.

The intercultural dimension of this language, in itself, is an important element for its emergence as a symbolistic instrument of wider communication.

4.1.1 American and British Influence—'A perfect play of politics and economics'

In the past, the British were the world rulers and with their supremacy came the proliferation of their language, English. The dominant role played by Britain in the Industrial Revolution galvanized the position of the English language.

Though today the Americans have taken over and American culture is becoming everyone's second nature, yet the British still see a dash of hope of using the English language to re-establish their lost glory, which they had earned during their exploration and colonization days.

The geographical extent to which English spread across the globe is majorly governed by political factors exerted by the British colonialism during the 19th century. But what sustained and fed this spread were the dramatic boom cycles and economic influence exerted by the American economy in the 20th century. American English has grown steadily in international importance since World War II. It is during this same period that the importance of languages like French declined.

These two key historical factors breathed life into English. It is the perfect interplay of political and economic factors that has made English what it is today.

4.1.2 Working Knowledge—'English will help you swim across the knowledge ocean'

Working knowledge is one of the tools for fulfilling personal as well as global needs in the eco-socio-cultural context. People all over the world have come to depend on English for their well-being. They are aware of the current scenario and its requirements.

As working knowledge of English is required in most fields, education departments and councils across the world have already mandated or are in the process of instituting policies for the inclusion of English in the education syllabus. Those who strive to make a mark in their discipline and aspire to attain world recognition need the knowledge of English.

With English-driven knowledge growing at unprecedented rates, higher education systems need to equip future professionals with the ability to grasp and utilize this vast sea of knowledge. Mere domain knowledge of a particular field is not good enough by itself. What matters the most is the ability to learn, unlearn and re-learn, and that too in English. Constant upgrades in the level of English proficiency provide insurance against the ups and downs of the rapidly changing economic environment.

One of the most effective ways of improving your working knowledge is using the English language 'outside the classroom'. Classroom learning is the base, but to maintain and strengthen this base, practical application and experience is a requisite.

The working knowledge of English gives you the ability to work productively and maintain effective working relationships with colleagues of different national and cultural backgrounds.

Professionals who are leaders in their respective fields have learned how to use English to develop the power to attract. Finally, leadership in any field is about making people follow you and your agenda. With your working knowledge arsenal, you can develop the art of persuasion and establish credibility amongst others.

4.1.3 Information Revolution—'A new world order'

Today, the information age has replaced the industrial age. Information Revolution has redefined the world map; it has diffused economic and geographic boundaries. This new world order has opened the door to more opportunities of information movement and integration, and English is the main vehicle for materializing these opportunities to provide the rich bandwidth of global growth and gradual adaptability to a surplus of information.

As the society at large converges, so does language. English is the heart of this convergence. With people becoming more culturally and linguistically diverse and tolerant, convergence of cultures is on the rise, and to fuel this rise, information revolution is a crucial component. This revolution has resulted in an outpouring of English words and phrases, which allow us to describe new concepts or reshape old concepts to meet modern day perceptions.

English is a major part of this information revolution. With English on your side, this revolution becomes a much more enriching experience. Today, our relationships are no longer one-dimensional, rather they span across nations both through physical contacts and cyber communities, thanks to the role played by English in the Information Revolution. It is about creating networks of communities to help them achieve shared objectives.

Spotlight

Improving your English and that too in the right way, is the best investment you can make, which will generate huge dividends (information, knowledge) in all spheres of your life. Thanks to the role played by English in the new world order—Information Revolution.

The Information Revolution has a decentralizing yet integrating effect in terms of information power, and with English, this power over information can be much more widely distributed. This combination creates unlimited communication. English as the most popular language of this revolution empowers us to initiate direct participation as "global citizens" in global campaigns, agreements and initiatives—climate change, border treaties, peace process, human rights, trade agreements, international instability, social and economic justice, and global warming. It builds a holistic focus within people; people learn to approach both nearby, near-term issues and deeper, distributed issues.

This new world order is opening several transnational communication links to many millions of speakers across the globe. Geo-political forces will continue to play a major role in the world, but with this new world order, they will need to share the stage with people who possess "soft power—information".

4.2 Various Industries—'Everyone Wants to be a Global Market Player'

> English is the difference
> Between success and failure—
> It makes the future of the business world brighter.

English influences E-commerce transactions, global mergers, global acquisitions, modern literature, arts, technological advances and scientific developments, and vice versa.

Finally, at the end of the day, the teams of each and every organization are its main marketing department. If they are able to understand English and also be understood in English, and that too without a hint of difficulty, then half the battle of business entities is won.

All industries want to become global market players. They want to establish a large footprint in the world profits. Their main aim is to establish an international market for their products and services. Nearly all of the world's international business is done in English. And these goals are possible only when the industry entities and professionals are well-versed in English.

> **A Word of Caution**
>
> The 'noticeable' gap in Spoken and Written English is a major cause of concern for business houses. Apart from the investment in training programs for business specific skills, attitudes and domain knowledge, organizations need to pay equal attention towards the enhancement of skills in English.

In the corporate space, English is used for international communication, cross-country conferences, top management meetings and high-level negotiations. In current times of cut-throat economic competition, what will keep your organization ahead in the game, is the international influence of English to meet the future needs of both internal and external customers.

Learning Business English pertains not only to the speaking aspect of business correspondence. But it also includes methods and techniques of being able to deliver technically correct business presentations, strike profitable deals, handle negotiations effectively and all sorts of communication, be it written, spoken or in electronic format.

In today's world of collaborative team culture, it is a must to have English in your skills toolkit. When several teams present on several locations, need to collaborate in order to produce the desired results and provide excellent customer service, proficiency in English plays a critical role here.

Several countries have come to realize that a workforce proficient in English is the key to building the country as an international center for business.

With so many plus points of English, we all should look at it as an incentive for us to contribute in the development of our world.

4.3 Monopoly as the Worldwide Medium of Communication—'The Portal of Intellectuality'

Communicating in English
Is a rewarding experience.
It is not just a language, but also
An ideological movement, shining in brilliance.

English and its monopoly as the worldwide medium of communication is a favorite topic in academia and throughout the world. The knowledge of this language has been recognized as one of the key driving forces in the 21st century.

People accept English with open arms. Over the years, the world has come to realize that learning this language is a lifelong investment and a major intellectual capital gain. It is the language most commonly used and understood by almost all countries. One of the most important reasons for this popularity is that English definitely reduces the cultural gaps, if not wholly but substantially.

As the official language of international organizations and forums like United Nations (UN), United Nations Educational, Scientific and Cultural Organization (UNESCO), English serves as a unified forum for each nation and organization to present itself to the world. In fact, UN has six official languages, but most of its operations are carried out in English. English is also the working language of the economic and geo-political organization, the Association of Southeast Asian Nations (ASEAN). Apart from these, many prominent scientific organizations and international alliance bodies hold talks in English only.

In international bodies where several nations are members, the situation becomes complex due to translation/interpretation scenarios. The number of language pairs involved is high, and it is difficult to find experts for translating and interpreting these language pairs. One of the most viable alternatives for such a difficult situation is that of an intermediary language. Here again, the 'first' choice is English.

One may think that English is the first choice only in USA, UK or Asian nations. Well, this fact applies to Europe too. English is the pivotal force, which can make or break the state of affairs, international relations and cultural ties.

> **Spotlight**
>
> You are NEVER too old to learn a new language, including English. In order to keep ahead of the game, start NOW!
>
> Whatever you are currently into, either education or profession, sooner or later you will see that only those people who can strike a polished conversation, make great presentations, participate in meetings and negotiate in English will survive and succeed.

Once you become an expert in English, you will be able to:

(a) Negotiate well
(b) Communicate well
(c) Listen to the big picture
(d) Resolve conflicts
(e) Focus on issues, not people
(f) Win people's cooperation and trust
(g) Deal with problems effectively
(h) Establish a great rapport with people
(i) Project a confident self-image
(j) Find common ground
(k) Be open to other's ideas and views
(l) Use your voice effectively
(m) Feel proud of the communicative power you have at your disposal

Do not look at this monopoly as a means of losing your own identity. Rather look at it in terms of bilingualism—English provides you with opportunities for achieving global presence and your own language (if other than English) is a symbol of your identity.

4.3.1 How Important is English to You: A Survey

I conducted a survey with a mix of people—both native and non-native speakers of English. The total number of survey participants was 150. These belonged to various fields of professions and cultures. The following simple questions were asked to each of the participants and then a percentage figure was derived for the responses.

(a) How crucial is the knowledge of English to advance in your career?
   (i) 92 per cent said it is crucial
   (ii) 6 per cent said it is important but not mandatory
   (iii) 2 per cent responded with not at all

(b) How much time, you think, will you need to achieve a high proficiency level in English?
   (i) 4 per cent—4 years and above
   (ii) 16 per cent—between 2 to 4 years
   (iii) 45 per cent—1 year
   (iv) 25 per cent—1 to 2 years
   (v) 10 per cent—less than a year

(c) How far, you think, will learning English benefit students in their lives?
   (i) 89 per cent responded with English will benefit students in all spheres of life
   (ii) 7 per cent said it is beneficial but not critical
   (iii) 4 per cent responded in negation

(d) How successful are you in deducing the meanings of words from their context?
   (i) 60 per cent responded with successful sometimes
   (ii) 23 per cent said successful most of the times
   (iii) 17 per cent responded always

(e) How often do you use suitable verbal as well as non-verbal means of expression?
   (i) 71 per cent responded with not so often
   (ii) 25 per cent said sometimes
   (iii) 4 per cent responded with often

Conclusion: Though the last two questions show a poor level of English fluency, yet from responses to the first three questions (a to c), we can conclude that the majority of the respondents realize the importance of English and are willing to invest time and efforts in order to bridge the gaps and improve their quality of being accomplished in English skills.

4.4 Views and Attitudes Towards English—'Mainly Positive'

A positive attitude
Towards English
Helps you to exude
Great confidence.

According to the *Macmillan English Dictionary* (2002), the word attitude is defined as "someone's opinions or feelings about something, especially as shown in their behavior". This holds good for languages too.

One of the most common views of looking at the English language is that it welcomes influences from other languages. Both students and teachers look at it as a way of building a secular and cosmopolitan culture.

(a) *Sampling design*

The subjects (total 45) of my study were all in the age group of 18-24 years. They were students of various streams, right from economics to software engineering and from law to architecture.

(b) *Findings*

Out of 45 people that I interviewed, 39 affirmed that the benefits one derives after learning English is one of the main motivating factors for learning this language. The attitudes and responses were analyzed on the basis of motivation levels, social context, cultural background and future aspirations.

It has been admitted by 90 per cent of the respondents that they do have plans of taking up professional courses in English. They strongly believe that knowledge of the language will help them shape their future. In fact, all the 45 respondents showed equal respect for their own mother language as well as English (a positive sign).

The six most important motivators identified in the survey are: Personality enhancement, better job prospects, to rise above peer pressure, higher education levels, higher self-esteem, and to be a part of the western culture and the global village. The numbers in the 'Number' column indicate the number of people who gave a particular rank (1 to 6) to the factors. The total of the Number column does not add up to 45 as many participants ascribed the same rank to more than one motivator. Most number of votes went to the overall personality enhancement factor followed by better job prospects and the rest.

Table 4.1: Views and Attitudes towards English Survey Summary

Rank #	Motivator Description	Number
1	To enhance personality on all levels	45
2	To increase self-confidence and self-esteem	42
3	To secure better job prospects	41
4	To compete with peer pressure	39
5	To achieve higher Education levels	39
6	To feel English, to be a part of the western culture and the global village	38

With the above figures, we can safely conclude that the English language is of paramount importance in the academic and professional lives of people. Findings from several previous surveys reveal that an immigrant who speaks English well earns 33 per cent more than an immigrant who speaks English poorly, and a person who speaks English very well earns 67 per cent more.

Language attitudes are changing all the time, and especially in a positive sense, when it comes to English. The more positive attitudes people have towards the English language, the better they relate to it and its advantages.

If proficiency in English is to improve on a global level, each one of us needs to play our part well:

(a) Government authorities and councils need to provide the necessary infrastructure, facilities and finances for setting up English language departments and courses.

(b) Educational institutions must have the right kind of policies and methods for imparting knowledge in this language, and developing the critical and creative thinking skills of the students through this language.

(c) Parents need to support and encourage their children to take up English as a language.

(d) Students need to realize that English is a key driver in achieving excellence in all aspects of life.

(e) Professionals should be aware of the fact that English is the roadmap to career growth.

(f) General masses, social groups, newspapers and media must support all that is done for building an English-driven society.

The bottom line is that innovative approaches to learning and teaching are needed so that this innovation thrives on itself in order to produce effective changes and more innovations in the process.

4.4.1 The Importance of Feeling English—'Feel the Essence of English'

Some people focus entirely on their professional growth and academic pursuits, least realizing the importance of feeling and knowing English. They feel that mere hard work will help them overcome all hurdles. In reality, a combination of diligence and English will help them scale newer heights of success.

A Word of Caution

The word 'Chartered Accountant' in British English is equivalent to 'CPA (certified public accountant)' in American English. Imagine writing a business proposal in British English and sending it to an American counterpart using the term Chartered Accountant. What a confusion it will create!

You cannot speak English fluently unless and until you feel the essence of English. You need to mold yourself into the cast of the language that you are using.

Not feeling English, may land you in trouble. For example, the British and Americans have different spellings, different pronunciations and also different words for the same business term.

You can never learn everything that exists in this world in one go. Learning is a lifelong experience. Whether you are graduating from high school or from college, learning must go on. This is where the importance of 'feeling' English comes into play. Once you realize that learning English is not merely about grammar or vocabulary, but it is also about the process of 'Enrichment', success will automatically follow you. Reading English books on literature, philosophy and history will make you well-informed as you get to learn about the various aspects of our world.

One of the probable reasons why people fear to converse or write without any inhibition is social rejection. They tend to be overcautious in social situations. They do not like to draw attention to themselves. They fear being embarrassed or misunderstood. They fear not being able to understand what people say to them in another language. Such people have much more difficulty practising and learning a foreign language than people who are more willing to speak up and less bothered by making a 'mistake' in another language.

Another major reason why people are not fluent is the approach towards English learning and teaching; it has an exam-centric focus. English is taught with an aim of ensuring that students do well in exams. We need to take it beyond the world of classroom to the world without walls. We need to teach and learn English with a purpose of preparing people for effective communication in various contexts of interaction.

We all are aware of the fact that learning any new skill is a challenging task. It needs incessant determination and not intermittent, non-focused bouts of learning. In my opinion, the **Five Rs** are the main factors that will help in instilling the 'Feeling English' factor within the English learning community and build incessant commitment towards the cause of acquiring an array of skills related to this language.

The Five Rs are as follows:

- Rock steady family support

  The parents of students need to support and understand the efforts of their children who are learning English. They need to value their child's learning efforts. Parental awareness and buy-in is a must. It is when parents express their firm belief that learning English is important for their child's future, the learning curve will be progressive in nature. According to Cotton and Wikelund (2007), "programs which involve parents in reading with their children, supporting their work on homework assignments, or tutoring them using materials and instructions provided by teachers show impressive results".

- Relentless efforts

  The learners need to sustain a positive attitude towards their language learning process. Visualize yourself achieving your language goals. Your efforts are needed both for the actual learning and for making time everyday for this learning. Self-discipline is the key to learning.

  Fluency and accuracy come with constant practice. These two aspects can be achieved only when a person is convinced about the advantages of English. No one can help a person to learn English devotedly than his own convinced mind.

  Firstly, listen to anything you can, and often. Secondly, talk, talk and talk. Thirdly, write, write and write. Fourthly, apply all that you learn without any fear. Relentless efforts are about moving forward in a balanced fashion.

- Resourceful motivators

  Motivating factors in the form of the need for knowledge, bright prospects, better future and success rate, and social competency combined with the other 'Rs' instill learning persistence in the learners. This in turn also increases the success rate in learning. Once the learners develop confidence in their own ability to grasp English, they are likely to approach new learning goals and tasks with a higher degree of enthusiasm. These motivators build new skills upon their experiential foundation.

- Robust education policies and practices

  The educational framework should provide efficient means of imparting education and invest wisely in teachers-training. Apart from human resources, there needs to be adequate access to the latest ways of learning English. Each and every student must have access to 'comprehensible and high-interest learning inputs and material' in the form of audio/video material, Internet content, journals and library resources.

- Role models in the form of parents, teachers

  A trusting relationship between role models and the learners is absolutely crucial, only then students will put in their best to meet the role models' expectations. Teachers and parents need to understand the personalities of the learners, their learning goals, prior literacy levels, and interests. Accordingly, these role models can design and apply learning methods and strategies.

  If one does not feel strongly for English, one is less likely to master it. Remember, apart from the soft skills, business know-how and domain knowledge, what sets you apart is your ability to communicate well using English.

4.5 Lesson 3—'Half Knowledge is Dangerous'

Illustration 4.1: Half Knowledge is Dangerous

Half knowledge is dangerous; the illustration exemplifies this very quote. One *out-of-place* word in the message can send out a stream of question marks and confused expressions. As you see in this illustration, the word 'values' (which actually should be valuables) has got the lady all confounded. She knows that the desk clerk means valuables, but for a second, she does think as to how she is going to leave her values of honesty and truthfulness at the front desk.

Some more bloopers caused by the half knowledge syndrome:

Coffee and Snakes—A sign in a coffee shop

Friend Eggs—A dish name in the menu

Open those windows. Let the air force come in.—Spoken by a non-native English speaker

4.6 Questions for Reflection

1. Do you think Americanization and the widespread presence of English is good for the future world?
2. How can you practise speaking when you are alone?
3. How would you rate the following statements on a scale of 1 to 3—1: Totally Agree, 2: Partially Agree, 3: Totally Disagree
    - English destroys the sense of patriotism.
    - Proficiency in English makes the activities involving English more enjoyable—reading magazines, conversing with native speakers.
    - Knowledge of English gets you praise and admiration from your family, relatives, friends and colleagues.
4. How does English make you a more culturally literate person?
5. What do you understand by the phrase 'comprehensible and high-interest learning inputs'?
6. What do we have to take into consideration when people from various cultures use English in global communication scenarios?

4.7 Chapter Recap

A. English is our 'Window to the World'—we live in an age of Information Technology. Through this window, we have several avenues at our disposal, which help to keep ourselves abreast of all the latest happenings in any part of the world.

B. There are five main aspects that make English the 'World Language'—geographic spread, number of users, the volume of information generated and disseminated, special status and the number of fields it affects.

C. It is interesting to note that English speakers and nations which were once colonized by this language are not just passively absorbing the language; they are actively reshaping and remaking it.

D. English influences E-commerce transactions, global mergers, global acquisitions, modern literature, arts, technological advances and scientific developments, and vice versa.

E. As the official language of international organizations and forums like United Nations (UN), United Nations Educational, Scientific and Cultural Organization (UNESCO), English serves as a unified forum for each nation and organization to present itself to the world.

F. When several teams present on several locations, need to collaborate in order to produce the desired results and provide excellent customer service, proficiency in English plays a critical role here.

G. The 'noticeable' gap in Spoken and Written English is a major cause of concern for business houses. Apart from the investment in training programs for business specific skills, attitudes and domain knowledge, organizations need to pay equal attention towards the enhancement of English skills.

H. One of the most common views of looking at the English language is that it welcomes influences from other languages. Both students and teachers look at it as a way of building a secular and cosmopolitan culture.

I. Some people focus entirely on their professional growth and academic pursuits, least realizing the importance of feeling and knowing English. They feel that mere hard work will help them overcome all hurdles. In reality, a combination of diligence and English will help them scale newer heights of success.

J. You cannot speak English fluently unless and until you feel the essence of English. You need to mold yourself into the cast of the language that you are using.

K. The Five Rs—rock steady family support, relentless efforts, resourceful motivators, robust education policies and practices, and role models help in enhancing your interest in this language.

PART-II

Beyond the Beginnings

Educational Equity—'A Symbol of Dreams and Aspirations'

5

Educational equity,
When backed by educational equality
And English teaching polices,
Is bound to become quality-driven.

It is true that language-related planning and policies need to be closely associated with the linguistic character of a particular region or country. But it is equally true that Education of a predominant language like English gets a *central* place in the education system. English is now the language most widely taught as a foreign language, and in several countries, it has already replaced other languages as the main foreign language to be taught in non-native speaking countries.

Educational equity is the backbone of the development of society and English plays a major role in strengthening this backbone. Going by the current standards of information dissemination, it is clearly evident that countries with high knowledge power combined with economic stability will be the forerunners. And with the advent of the Internet and its main language being English, it is pointless in being insular to the influence of global communication. Due to widespread dissemination of information, the language is no longer an exclusive property of its native speakers in the field of education. No wonder, the English language teaching industry is a multi-billion dollar industry today.

Today, English is not just looked at as yet another language. English is a process of empowerment in itself, through which people are able to secure a better quality of life. Mastering of English is as important as food, air and water to each one of us.

Whether you are a student considering various study options, a teacher interested in professional growth, or a dean of an educational institute interested in developing an English-friendly curriculum, you know that English is considered the passport to a bright and secure future. It is learnt as the principal foreign language in most schools in Western Europe. There is a growing demand for it in countries like China and Japan as well.

Earlier, non-native students enrolled in overseas educational institutions only if they were assured of a scholarship. Now, they are willing to support their education even if there are no scholarship options available as banks are providing educational loans at attractive interest rates.

In order to sustain and enhance Educational Equity, we need to invent ways of stirring an interest for English in the student community. The complexity of the classroom scenarios and the needs of the students should be recognized before embarking on the education programs.

In times to come, only those nations will be powerful who possess not only a strong economy or wield a major political influence, but also have a stronghold in the information field. This is possible only with the knowledge of English, in all areas—spoken, written, listening, critical thinking, and analytical skills.

A Word of Caution

Tips for students for building a strong base in English. BASICS matter a lot!

Analyze the methods, approach and the course materials employed in the English language degree, course or program. Cross-check on the availability of resources which focus on the basics too.

Do not ever learn English from a tutor who is not professionally qualified to teach in this language.

What matters the most in looking at this aspect are the attitudes of people towards English as the new world order. If people look at this linguistic dominance with fear, then obviously they are not going to take it very well. Any global positive change must begin from within, and this is possible by building the right attitudes within people.

The main component that will help in building the right, healthy attitude towards English is the right kind of delivery approach of imparting the knowledge of English. We need to go beyond the typical rote learning mode in order to help people appreciate and imbibe the rich 'wordsworth' world of English.

In countries like Japan and China, teaching English has become a national mission. As more and more people are immigrating to English-speaking lands, the demand for both ESL and EFL programs is increasing too.

The demand is not only limited to learning English as a subject, but also includes learning other subjects in English. The focus is towards content and language integrated learning approaches. Several countries like Mexico, South Korea have launched large scale programs of teaching through English.

5.1 Academic Contexts—'A Unified Knowledge Platform'

English is the hub
Of academic conferences.
Plug into this hub
To gain knowledge across ages.

Brilliant research papers and amazing breakthroughs are useless, unless they are communicated to the intended audience in precise terms. When using English for academic purposes, it is important to be accurate both in speaking and writing in order to facilitate effective knowledge pooling.

According to Swales (1987), more than 50 per cent of the millions of academic papers published each year are written in English, and the percentage has been growing year after year ever since.

Every year a large number of academic conferences in various subjects are hosted across the globe and that too in English. One of the main reasons for English being the language of academic conferences is to move beyond the limits of traditional disciplinary boundaries, and provide a single platform to explore the relationships among different subjects and ways of integrating ground-breaking new research.

These academic conferences provide rich exposure to various subjects. With English as the standard, they also grant opportunities for intellectual pursuits.

When Spanish scientists want to share their new finds with the world scientific community, they share their discoveries both in English and their language.

Consider the case of an Italian student who is a bright spark and is really interested in research-oriented subjects like Bio-Technology. Then the best place for him to be is probably United States. But for him to survive there, he will need to learn English so that he can have access to research-oriented material, and also be able to exchange information with fellow researchers and scholars. Just imagine how much his prospects will increase ...*manifold*.

Advancement in the academic arena is a fundamental factor in the development of human beings, and for this advancement, we need qualified education in English.

5.2 English as a Second Language—'A Skill to be Valued'

English is a skill to be valued;
With it in your skill set,
Your world-view will be renewed.

Speaking more than one language is very common these days. In the area of second language acquisition, what is most important to note is that mere fluency should not be its only aim; this acquisition must also lead to communicative competence.

Despite the growing awareness of the importance of learning English, the level of proficiency in English among students is still a performance gap. A mere degree in any field will not get you the desired job and scope for growth. Time has changed and so have the views of the entire student community across the globe. They have come to realize that the only way to survive the cut-throat global competition is proficiency in English. There is an ongoing need for intensive courses in English as a Second Language (ESL), also known as English as a

Foreign Language (EFL) and English for Speakers of Other Languages (ESOL).

These days, there are endless options available to enroll in English as a second language courses. What makes these courses more accessible is the introduction of the Internet. Internet provides viable alternatives to register for ESL courses online. Modern methods of teaching and learning in the form of satellite education, video conferencing and virtual schools have opened up avenues for specialized courses for various professional fields.

Apart from ESL focus on professional growth, it also encompasses courses which are needed by students to clear exams like TOEFL (Test of English as a Foreign Language), IELTS (International English Language Testing System) in order to secure admission in top-notch universities.

The student world has become vigilant enough to realize that English is a must have in their educational toolkit to be able to reap the myriad of benefits of this 'Era of Knowledge'.

The international character of the English language is a primary reason for having it introduced in educational institutions. The primary purpose of ESL courses is to make an individual proficient in the use of the English language. The other main objectives of English education are:

1. To develop the skills of reading, writing, listening, critical thinking, communicating and negotiating.
2. To ensure that the learners are able to face the stiff competition in the international job market.
3. To relate to global social interaction contexts and patterns, and adjust interactions accordingly.
4. To meet future needs and aspirations through the knowledge of English as a foreign language/second language.
5. To provide opportunities for acting as responsible cosmopolitan citizens.
6. To instill the habit of sharing and accepting new values, validating and propagating new theories, and strengthening cultural identity.

7. To instill a sense of empathy, awareness of and sensitivity to cultural differences. To enable the learners to see the plus points in other cultures and value systems as well.
8. To develop understanding of communication strategies of other cultures and global communication.

As you can notice that these objectives do not only pertain to learning English as a language but also their scope entails building the right kind of attitudes and cognitive skills. It is not only the duty of education ministries, councils and boards to design effective approaches for both learning and teaching English. But both students and teachers should also work on building a sustainable approach.

ESL courses are not merely 'curriculum-based' courses or taught for achieving a particular job or securing admission in a particular college. They are aimed at imparting knowledge of English for developing intellectual and cognitive skills so that students turn out to be thorough professionals in all fields.

Spotlight

English teaching should be a lateral effort as opposed to a top down approach. This approach facilitates an increased engagement of students in their own learning, and the creation of a network of dedicated policymakers and educators.

The new concept of dedicated full-time second language/ foreign language schools in the third world countries in particular, is a clear depiction of their desire to excel, grow and contribute to the global dynamics.

Your decision to learn English as a second language could easily prove to be the most lucrative decision of your life. This is definitely going to turbo-charge your social as well as professional spheres. Bonne chance! Well, you must be wondering why I am using French. I am learning French these days. It is good to be multilingual. I have English, Marathi, Hindi and German in my language toolkit, and French will join in soon. If you are good in your mother tongue, then think of adding more languages to your languages repository, particularly English.

No language is easy or difficult to learn. What is required to flex our linguistic muscles are the right attitude, motivating factors, research-based practices, robust policies and dedicated mentors. Educational institutes in several Asian countries like Philippines and Korea have made it a point to hire native English speakers to educate students properly in English.

> **A Word of Caution**
>
> If you are planning to embark on the journey of English learning, don't set un-planned and lofty goals. One of the best ways to gain insights and inputs is from people who have been there done that, who have already invested planning, time and effort in mastering the art. Base your milestones on these inputs, instead on random guesstimates.

5.3 Lesson 4—'Fluency and Communicative Competence is a Must'

Illustration 5.1: Fluency Combined with Communicative Competence is a Must

In the illustration, the troubled man in the chair knows that he has a sore throat, but due to the lack of fluency and communicative competence, he says: 'I have sore trout', least knowing that his lack of proper pronunciation and the lack of grammar, vocabulary and syntax resulted in saying the word trout, which actually is a type of fish. No wonder, this evoked a startled reaction from his colleague.

Once you know the answers to the following questions:

- What words and grammatical structures do I use for the given settings, people and their beliefs, attitudes, socio-cultural background and views?
- How to ask questions, deliver a speech, put up an argument, make a request, etc.?
- What tactics and mechanisms of this language do I use to create effective e-mails, powerful presentations, engaging conversations, etc.?
- How to use the words to contribute effectively to both formal and informal settings?
- What do I do if I have used the wrong terms or have conveyed a misinterpreted message?

You will not only produce language correctly, but also use it effectively for a particular purpose.

5.4 Students and their Perspective—'We are the Future'

We are the world,
We are the future,
And in paving the path to this future
We need English as a co-partner.

Economic growth of a nation and the quality of Education are directly related. When the quality of instruction is poor, not only do students suffer but also the overall growth of a nation is negatively affected. This in turn leads to widening of the chasm between the poor and the rich. As the rich have access to resources for learning English, they become even richer. One of the most effective ways of avoiding this elitism is to introduce well-resourced education policies at the school level itself. I believe in the concept of 'earlier the better'. It is proven empirically that children learn new concepts, skills and languages faster than adults. And this quick language acquisition at an early age will help everyone to influence their lives positively.

We need to find ways to ensure that students continue developing their skills in English, even outside the classroom scenario. It is essential to ensure that students are convinced that English is not just a language to get great grades, but a vehicle which helps to enrich the overall personality.

With Internet on our side, we can definitely hone our skills in English, *effectively*. With a simple click of the mouse, one can enter the world of online learning material and resources in the form of presentations, interactive games, speaking practice forums, e-books, radio programs, discussion forums, journals, quizzes, magazines and support groups. You name it and you get access to it. For example, sites such as YouTube contain many video lessons and presentations on English. There are also specialized journals available for the same.

Spotlight

Research figures show that children having a bi-linguistic or multi-linguistic skill set have higher achievement levels than children who are English-only or Mother-tongue only students.

5.4.1 Students and their attitudes towards English survey

(a) *Sampling design*

The study (total 150) I conducted with class 8 and 9 grade students over a period of two months reveals some interesting facts.

(b) *Survey objectives*

The objective of the survey was to create a profile of the students in terms of their attitudes towards English. The main objective of this survey was to analyze their perspective towards the various aspects of English.

(c) *Data analysis and findings*

I asked the following questions to these students—How do you perceive English:

- As a language for communication
- Usage in the classroom
- Usage outside the classroom
- In the spoken form
- Grammar
- Pronunciation
- In the written form
- Vocabulary

The table given below shows that overall response was positive with a minor 8 per cent accounting for the category of negative response, and only 2 per cent belonging to the 'neutral' and 'not sure' categories each.

Table 5.1: Perceptions of Students towards English

Factor	*Positive*	*Negative*	*Neutral*	*Not Sure*
English as a Language	148	1	0	1
Use of English inside the classroom	148	1	1	0
Use of English outside the classroom	148	2	0	0
Speaking	148	2	0	0
Grammar	145	3	1	1
Pronunciation	147	1	1	1
Writing	149	1	0	0
Vocabulary	149	1	0	0

Why English? The following direct quotes from the students belonging to the positive category indicate that students of modern era know what they want out of the English language:

> "The English language is an essential prerequisite to perform well at the workplace."
>
> "It helps me to take decisions based on reference to the wider world."
>
> "To be able to absorb and keep pace with the ever-increasing knowledge explosion and technology boom."
>
> "To have better prospects in the professional space. English also opens the door to global exposure."
>
> "To be able to relate to the western culture and adjust to its ways."

"It enables me to communicate with cogency and precision on a global level."

"It helps me to keep myself abreast of the latest developments in the fields of space technology, satellite communication and the like."

"I want to become a great scientist, and for doing so, I need to be good at English. As most scientific journals and research papers in any school or university library are aimed at an international readership, thus they are published in English."

"I want a good software job. To work with computers, English is a necessity."

"English will help me make it big." (I think this particular response sums up all the previous responses.)

5.4.2 Study abroad, progress in foreign lands—'A new journey and a ticket to high leverage'

Studying abroad is one of the main ways of securing the future needs of younger minds. The key driver of the 21st century academic revolution is English. Academic mobility is another hallmark of the English language. And one needs to capitalize on this mobility in order to meet the challenging needs of the global age.

Technological advancements have now made learning English much more easy, creative and convenient. Conversation groups are an excellent tool for improving English. These are organized by international student offices, English-language centers, academic departments and public libraries. Alternatively, students can form their own study groups and discussion forums too. While learning English, the Internet is your best friend.

> **Spotlight**
>
> The right mix of up-to-date learning material, textbooks and methods definitely ensures the creation of intellectual assets.

Students who study abroad always say that they experience growth in all spheres of life—professional, cultural, intellectual, social and personal. Though their main aim is to master the

English language, students feel that this aim is in a way introducing them to a whole new world, to a whole new culture altogether. Another major gain from their international sojourn is broader horizons and deepened knowledge of global economics, politics and other international issues.

Leaving your own homeland and going abroad (USA, UK, etc.) is a life-changing step and many challenges await new immigrants in nations where English is the main language. Apart from the cultural shock and several other factors, one of the main challenges is that of overcoming the language barrier.

There are several immigrants who can speak English well, but this skill is majorly influenced by their local teaching policies, their upbringing and their own environment. More than the language, what matters is the way it is spoken. To overcome this baggage of challenges, it is imperative for one to not only learn this language, but also speak it the way it is supposed to be spoken in the foreign land.

Monoglot English students are bound to fall back in the race, as qualified multilingual students have an edge due to their fluency in English along with their mother tongues. Additional language capabilities are definitely a plus.

Multilingual students and professionals have come to realize that English-speaking is regarded as the *ticket* to social and economic advancement.

Education for overseas students has become a major industry in many countries and is growing faster than most other service industries.

A Word of Caution

Don't look at TOEFL or IELTS scores as mere résumé adornments. Keep in mind the goals you want to achieve and then work hard towards attaining them.

5.4.3 TOEFL—'From here to anywhere and everywhere'

TOEFL stands for Test of English as a Foreign Language. It is a requirement for non-native English speakers to secure university and college admissions. It comes in two flavors—written and computer-based. I am sure many of you have already gone through the grind of preparation. Unlike other tests, TOEFL evaluates listening, reading, speaking and writing skills, and tests the aspirants' ability to combine two or more of these skills too.

Excellent scores in TOEFL alone are not the best criteria for judging one's language fluency. Additional tests to gauge the listening, writing and speaking ability are required. Potential students may either need to appear for an oral interview or are given a topic for essay writing.

The same practice holds good for aspiring English teachers. They may have to give a presentation and many a time, the audience for this presentation is none other than students. The main reason for such additional tests is to determine whether aspiring teachers have the capability to fulfill the duties and roles associated with the teaching field.

English is one way to land yourself a growth-driven job or shift to a better lifestyle. Whether you want to benefit from the IT boom or seek employment in the ever-expanding field of tourism, English is needed. Because English is more needed today than ever, the demand for TOEFL is growing.

> **A Word of Caution**
> Students lacking proficiency in English have much lower High school graduation rates.

5.5 Teachers' Perspective—'Facilitators of Learning'

English is a vast knowledge ocean,
which sets you in motion.
English is highly motivating,
which helps you in elevating.

Due to the new migration trends, globalization wave and changing student dynamics, education in general and teacher education in particular, needs to be constantly revised and reformed. Teachers are required to step out of their limited role of teaching; they need to act as facilitators of effective language development.

A combination of "engaged partnership" of teachers, school authorities and students, and "reflective teaching" is the best way to impart skills. This approach is definitely being welcomed more often these days. As far as the English language is concerned, teachers are more than just being teachers; they are slowly and steadily playing the role of mediators of education who connect learners to the world.

In order to support the above observations, I conducted a survey of 35 teachers of higher education over a period of two months. I found that 75 per cent had an experience base of more than 25 years while the rest had an experience base of less than 25 years. 85 per cent of the teachers were of the view that the number of students taking English has been on the rapid rise in the last few years and would continue to increase in the future too. Out of these 85 per cent, 80 per cent firmly believe that English and technology-based resources will dominate the education scene. All of them agreed that teachers themselves have to be perfectly trained in order to ensure that students become perfect in the subject, be it English, Mathematics or any other discipline.

In developing countries, the need for more and more students to be proficient in English is on the rise. Hence, qualified teachers of English are also highly sought after. Qualified no more means knowledge in terms of degrees or learning materials. Considering today's multicultural environment, teachers need to help students to acquire both the linguistic and cultural dimensions of learning English.

Teachers just like students are coming out of the typical role, and prefer to use more active learning methods. Out of the 35 teachers that I interviewed, 29 teachers said that they like to employ active learning techniques. They feel that these methods help in increasing student's interest, participation and interaction in the teaching-learning life cycle.

Teachers need to act as researchers to be able to build new and improved teaching practices, delivery processes and evaluation systems. Teachers have begun to realize that earlier English was taught to support basic life skills, but now it is more of a life support system in itself. Their changing *avatar* will not only provide them with the satisfaction of developing perfect students in English, but will act as an opportunity of professional growth too.

5.5.1 TESL—'Taking charge in the classroom'

Most teaching jobs abroad need at least a bachelor's degree for teaching ESL. More than mere teachers, they are agents of change.

The teachers should strive hard to improvise the teaching methodology. The main aim of Teaching English as a Second Language (TESL) is to train and perfect teachers as a medium of implementing the latest trends in English language teaching.

Over the years, the demand for English learning has increased manifold, whereas the supply of well-trained native English-speaking teachers is not able to keep up with it. With TESL in place, thousands of professionals can get a chance to travel abroad, to distant countries, and to earn a reasonably good living.

Spotlight

Teachers of English as a Second Language need to be aware of the various cross-cultural communication styles.

As a teacher of this language, ensure you perform a proper needs analysis of your students in order to adapt the learning methods and material to their needs and cultural backgrounds.

One important tip which will make you an effective mentor is that just do not teach English in terms of grammar, phonetics and pronunciation. Go beyond the veneer of this language. Understand that it is a vehicle of culture too. Teachers need to teach the students the significance of the cultural background of English. Without the knowledge of this cultural background, students will learn the language just for the sake of learning it.

Good teachers are role models and they have the ability to inspire their students to develop mastery of as well as a liking towards the English language, both in written and spoken form.

Teachers need to remember that students working together and their special interests being taken care of through need-based courses, make for a successful collective learning experience and self-confident usage of this language. Small classes ensure a high-level of individual attention.

5.6 Ways to Reach and Teach English

> The absolute best way
> To learn English is to
> Surround yourself with it everyday.

The need of many people to learn a second language has turned the English education field into a thriving industry. Understanding the broader role of higher education in a globalized world is the first step to defining constructive ways of building an English-driven world and maintaining the learning continuum beyond the classroom.

> **Spotlight**
> English learning for students should be a fun-filled exercise so as to help them grasp the language better.

Many methods for teaching English as a second language have been developed over the years. With the significance of learning a second language so loud and clear, the question becomes one of how to implement it. In order to ensure the success of English language degrees, courses and programs, several concrete steps need to be taken. Effective teaching practices should entail a variety of teaching methods, strategies, aids and approaches; some of them are as follows:

1. Traditional teaching is a teacher-centered environment and students learn the language through drill and practice. Traditional methods of delivering lectures can work wonders when these lectures are designed in such a way that students are not just bombarded with information, but are also provided with opportunities to influence the classroom dynamics.

   The compartmentalized structure of traditional teaching is breaking down slowly and steadily. These days, the classroom scenario is a combination of traditional and modern learning, rather than purely traditional. Traditional learning still has a place; it cannot be done away with. It is about blended learning in a seamless manner in order to achieve a holistic learning experience. The focus is shifting from passive and receptive towards active and participative.

2. A language lab is an audio or audio-visual installation used as an aid in language teaching. Language labs play an important role in language development. It is an environment where the finer aspects of the language like pronunciation and tenses can be well taught.
3. The direct method dictates that all language teaching and classroom instructions should occur in the target language only.
4. Internet-driven teaching-learning model is a feasible option as compared to regular degrees. There is a plethora of tools and E-resources for the various aspects of learning the English language. You name it and there are resources for it. There are forums where you can learn from native speakers. There are podcasts and videos streaming on various websites. Then there are instant communication tools like chats. The main advantage of a web-based method is that it is available all the time; it operates 24/7, 365 days a year.

   Virtual learning environments combined with the power of technology tools means that distance is no longer an impediment to finding a good language teacher. Today, interesting and comprehensible learning content on a varicty of aspccts of English is only a click away.
5. Differentiated instruction in classrooms is becoming popular today. Here, the teaching content, methods, materials, assignments, and even assessment and adjustment are based on the diverse learning styles, capabilities and needs of students.
6. Field experience is a real-life setting with an aim to help students to learn how to study, observe, participate in and react to real-life situations. Field experience also provides insights and cognitive challenges thereby providing viewpoints into the lives and cultures of others.

7. Constant exposure ensures that all aspects of English (listening, speaking, thinking, reading and writing) are not devalued. Constant exposure is all about 'thinking in English'; this helps to instill a solid habit of learning. Allowing the students to be creative and providing a practical environment also ensure constant exposure and sustained interest levels in the language.
8. Cooperative language learning is one of the most constructive teaching strategies. In traditional teaching, one will find either teacher-student interaction or student-initiated interaction, whereas in cooperative language learning student-student interaction is maximal. The students learn the language through group activities and interactions in order to achieve shared learning goals.

   Learners in the real world come in all shapes and sizes, exhibiting different personality traits and learning needs. Thus, a combination of methods, both traditional and modern, is required to cater to the three main learning needs of the learners—Kinesthetic, Visual and Auditory, and also to establish links to the learners' prior knowledge. This ensures that both the teachers and learners have a well-rounded, memorable and balanced teaching-learning experience.

A Word of Caution

Verbal refuse=Slang, mumbo-jumbo. Dump it into the dustbin as that is where it rightfully belongs.

5.7 Questions for Reflection

1. What are the costs and benefits of teaching English as a foreign language?
2. How can foreign language education contribute to the improvement of education?
3. What are your attitudes towards second language learning?
4. Can educational equity exist where there is no educational equality?

5. What are the reasons for learning a language?
6. Do the ethnicity and experience base of teachers affect their use of English in the classroom?
7. In what ways can motivation affect English language learning?
8. Is your university/college/school/language program ready for the surge in students aspiring to master the English language?

5.8 Chapter Recap

A. With the advent of Internet and its main language being English, it is pointless in being insular to the influence of global communication.

B. In order to sustain and enhance the Educational Equity, we need to invent ways of stirring an interest for English in the student community.

C. The main component that will help in building the right, healthy attitude towards English is the right kind of delivery approach of imparting the knowledge of English.

D. Brilliant research papers and amazing breakthroughs are useless, unless they are communicated to the intended audience in precise terms. When using English for academic purposes, it is important to be accurate both in speaking and writing in order to facilitate effective knowledge pooling.

E. One of the main reasons for English being the language of academic conferences is to move beyond the limits of traditional disciplinary boundaries, and provide a single platform to explore the relationships among different subjects and ways of integrating ground-breaking new research.

F. There is an ongoing need for intensive courses in English as a Second Language (ESL), also known as English as a Foreign Language (EFL) and English for Speakers of other Languages (ESOL).

G. It is essential to ensure that students are convinced that English is not just a language to get great grades, but a vehicle which helps to enrich the overall personality.

H. Economic growth of a nation and the quality of education are directly related. When the quality of instruction is poor, not only do students suffer but also the overall growth of a nation is affected negatively.

I. The main aim of TESL is to produce teachers as a medium of implementing latest trends in English language teaching.

J. Studying abroad is one of the main ways of securing the future needs of younger minds. The key driver of the 21st century academic revolution is English. Academic mobility is another hallmark of the English language.

K. Good teachers are role models and they have the ability to inspire their students to develop mastery of as well as a liking towards the English language, both in written and spoken form.

L. Constant exposure through both the traditional mode of teaching and Internet-driven teaching-learning model will help students to grasp the language, both faster and better.

6 Building a World Without Walls—'Welcome to the Collaboration Age'

A world without walls
Is a vision of integrating people,
For which English provides a platform, mutual.

To strike a common ground and to be well-rounded, respectful members of the world, English could be the most viable option. **Education, Peaceful Coexistence** and **Economic Growth** are three main pillars of international development.

The main reason for hurdles in these three aspects is *dilemmas of dialogue*. English provides the global voice to forge collaborative links in all spheres of life (economic, social, scientific, etc.), to integrate the efforts of peacemaking forums, to expand the intellectual and cultural horizons, and to negotiate a fair solution to global issues. English is the most important tie that binds us together on several levels, and builds a broad-minded cultural and linguistic perspective.

At the world level, conducting diplomatic talks and settling international issues needs English. The knowledge of this language helps to dissolve extreme views and attitudes that still hold a colonial connotation towards English, and break out of the ethnocentric shells.

English is one such language that gives full liberty to people, particularly non-native speakers, to explore its many facets based on their own cultural and linguistic experiences. This allows non-native speakers to add their own flavors to this language. This quality of English is what makes it a multicultural language.

One of the most compelling factors for the rise in demand for English is the fact that it not only enhances the individual domain, but also plays a dominant role in this globalized world, and helps to create hubs of language and cultural skills. By facilitating dialog to determine strategies for handling critical issues like nuclear treaty, environmental concerns, terrorism and poverty, it forges balanced partnerships between nations.

The main global objective is not just to compete in a healthy fashion, but also to cooperate with other cultures and nations to handle global challenges and shared concerns. Finally, it is about peace and harmony, only then the globalized community as a whole can succeed in all walks of life, right from cooperation alliances to commerce treaties. The English language is homogenizing and globalizing the world community at several levels.

When people will realize the importance of the following factors:

A. A conducive education system, where people from all walks of life come together to learn about each other through English,

B. A common platform/forum for voicing issues and finding solutions to bridge cultural gaps, and

C. A bias-free environment, where cultural values can be exchanged, studied, developed and imbibed.

They will also realize the importance of imbibing English for further progress of society and the world. No nation or group of people who want to progress further can rely on just one language. In order to establish a distinct place in this diverse world, we all need to understand and relate to this diversity and its dynamics, and English helps us to deal with this diversity and its dynamics, *effectually*.

6.1 A Seamless Learning Continuum—'A Great Way of Sharing'

To overcome the challenges of change,
A seamless learning continuum
Powered by the fuel of English
Is the perfect twosome.

Research findings have proved that knowledge of English hones the problem-solving skills, enhances creativity and sharpens the conceptualizing abilities. English is all about building transnational competencies. We have come a long way, from teaching English as a classroom subject to imbibing it as a life skill to survive in the global context. Our local tongues help us to deal with the 'WHAT' aspect of life, whereas English helps us to think about the 'HOW' too. English provides learning opportunities through real and significant situations.

We as policymakers, parents, teachers and learners need to be clear of the various performance indicators, which can be used to track this learning continuum. The purpose of these performance indicators is to achieve the following:

- Identify and categorize learning patterns, learning attitudes and learning behaviors in order to design effective policies.
- Track and analyze the progress of the learning curve based on several learning parameters in terms of writing, reading, phonological knowledge, communication level, etc.
- Validate prior learning and knowledge.
- Introduce the necessary changes to fill the learning gaps.

Several teachers that I met in various parts of the world said teaching English overseas is really a rewarding experience. And it is this enthusiasm of theirs that builds a stable network of learning resources.

English provides a seamless learning continuum not only for students of English, but also for teachers of English. Once you have been an ESL teacher for a year or so, then you can always move to another field where the knowledge of English is a must. This helps to broaden your scope of growth.

Communication in English is vital for passing on knowledge from one generation to the other thereby bridging the generational divide. This knowledge holds the key to future progress, and this is where English steps in to ensure that more and more people join the progress bandwagon through the communication links of knowledge.

A software engineer who is excellent in technology 'A' today, may have to learn technology 'B' tomorrow. This is necessary for him to keep abreast of the latest developments in his field. But what helps him in doing so, is his adeptness in English. English gives him the insurance cover against the vagaries of rapid changes. This language helps you to realize that learning is not only about technical or specialized education, it is about developing the intellectual capacity too.

> **Spotlight**
> English is all about Learning, Un-learning and Re-learning skills, technological expertise, tools, competencies, etc. Do not expect to understand everything at once. The point is to keep learning a new language fun and entertaining.

My most favorite way of improving English and maintaining the continuum is *quality* reading. It is shocking to note that the literacy rate in several native-speaking countries is falling. Many people do not read books anymore. They are more into instant entertainment and that too at the cost of education. Trust me, books, magazines, journals and encyclopedias can be both entertaining and educative...Edutainment! The most scholarly of all encyclopedias is the Encyclopedia Britannica. It is the oldest English-language encyclopedia still in print. You can call it the 'one stop shop' for all topics under the sun.

Because of a plethora of methods available for learning English, right from online dictionaries to social networking sites, the seamless learning continuum is heading towards convenience and comfort. This is resulting in more and more people joining the bandwagon, which means there is an insatiable appetite for knowledge from all four corners of the world. English gives its speakers the ability to use the language, and at the same time, impart information of interest to like-minded people. It also validates the experience and knowledge that people have.

English brings about the transformation of the wealth of knowledge from various domains into practical learning experiences. Factors like social interactions and discussions, and expression of our understanding of various aspects through sensory observation, help to construct and associate meaning to the world we live in. To develop this wider meaning, awareness and understanding, English is required. English acts as a springboard for integrating the intelligence of millions of minds thereby making this intelligence a seamless part of the learning continuum. This in turn helps us to move beyond the vision of "learning about knowledge" towards "learning knowledge itself".

For those who already speak the English language, going to another country for work/business won't be much of a problem in terms of communication. But for those whose first language is not English, it could pose a potential problem. When we have more and more people joining in, we can improve our English skills by learning from one another, through techniques like meaningful inquiry and collaboration. By challenging people to move out of their rigid comfort zone, English encourages people to be active agents in the learning continuum, which in turn encourages them to contribute actively to their community and nation.

6.1.1 Lesson 5—'Do not rush into learning the language'

Illustration 6.1: Do Not Rush into Learning the English Language

As you can see in the illustration, the taxi owner approaching us is all startled with the word 'taxed' on the sides of the other taxi. The bottom line is that do not rush into learning the language. Take it each step at a time. Do not follow any short cut, crash course methods.

Correct usage and the context matter a lot, or else a state of confusion is bound to arise. Factors like situational and cultural context need to be considered to break down barriers in the communication cycle.

Do not overload yourself. Learning a language is a process. Above all, make sure you are learning and improving a little bit every day.

6.2 A Seamless Corporate Culture—'A Key Asset'

A seamless corporate culture
Needs the backing of English
To build a bright future.

No nation that wants to deal with the rest of the world can rely on just its own language. Business houses which tend to play down the importance of the knowledge of English as an intellectual asset, lose a lot of opportunities. Corporations with a lot of respect for English, not only reap huge profits in their local markets, but are able to forge links with the global corporate culture too. Once organizations realize the importance of English, they will also understand how this language helps to understand their clients' culture in a better way. This understanding helps the employees to deliver the appropriate message to the clients, and in turn they succeed in making that 'Great First Impression'.

A nation's success in building a strong presence in the corporate space has often been attributed to the fact that majority of the professionals are educated in English. Mastery of English helps corporate houses to move beyond the limits of traditional operational boundaries. It is a *global formula* for exploring new ventures and building niche market areas.

> **Spotlight**
>
> My last trip to South-East Asia proved to be a beneficial one. It helped me to formulate a results-supported opinion about the importance of English. Through a series of discussions with several managers and leaders of top companies, I learned a lot of useful points regarding the importance of English.
>
> **Conclusion:** English enables us to incorporate international corporate cultural practices and build a constructive corporate culture. English is the competitive advantage needed to maintain a leading position in the corporate space.

Just as corporate culture and policies influence the level of English skills, in the similar manner, English plays a major role in inculcating proper business ethics and corporate culture. It gives the right visibility to position your business in international markets.

Learning the English language achieves the following corporate goals:

A. Awareness of foreign business culture and etiquettes.

B. Effective communication with internal as well as external customers in business.

C. Effective negotiation skills and hence better deals.

D. Better understanding of markets, and hence better strategies for designing the most suitable products and services.

E. Better understanding of multivendor environments and cross-functional teams in order to ensure business growth and continuity.

F. Your vocabulary mirrors your personality and success level. Business English builds word power and vocabulary competency.

G. Knowledge of international business practices.

In others words, everything has to be at the peak of perfection.

From the moment you see a great job advertisement, what all goes through your mind...here let me help you with it...a grilling interview, the day-to-day interactions with team members, high-end managerial talks, intensive meetings, action-packed brainstorming sessions and much more, and of course, one major question mark hanging like a sword of Damocles over your head: "how am I going to handle all this?" Believe me...all this is manageable with effective English communication skills. With the wand of English in your hand, you can swish away this sword of constant threat and uncertainty. Look at this challenge in a positive way—learning English is not just a simple addition to your skill set, but a major prerequisite needed to keep up with the fast changing trends.

Today, most companies in the world are tapping the mesh of outsourcing opportunities. This means, they are going to have to establish robust communication links with resources from other countries, and here too, English is the common factor.

6.2.1 Business Acronyms—'An integral part and parcel of work life'

Business acronyms are an integral component of corporate communication. They have a direct impact on your work, no matter where you are in the organizational chart.

Many businesses use English as their working language. Just like you can't eat sushi with a fork and knife, similarly, you can't do international business in any language other than English. Thus, it is imperative for employees to have knowledge of the related specialized vocabulary of their profession.

Every industry has its own acronyms and core vocabulary. To survive in your chosen field, not only will you need to know these acronyms in-depth, but will need to know the language in which these acronyms are—English. They are a part and parcel of your professional lives. English is necessary for building an international business-oriented language, developing a competent workforce and collaboration in the global community. Today, anyone who wants to play an impressive role in the international network, needs to have access to the activation code—E.N.G.L.I.S.H.

> **Spotlight**
>
> The next time you are at a street corner or at a news kiosk, be sure to pick up at least one English national/international business journal, magazine or periodical. Capture the new words, acronyms and expressions in your personal diary or notebook. Keep revisiting and revising them, until they become a part of your 'active' business vocabulary.

Why don't we have a little quiz to tickle the business part of your brains? Let us see how much you score. To make things simpler, I have given you certain words of the acronyms, all you need to do is fill in the blanks. If you read the book from cover to cover, you might find some of the answers here itself.

Ready? Here we go. All the best!

AC	= Actual —	PV	= — Value
ROI	= Return on —	USP	= Unique — Point
CEO	= Chief — Officer	VC	= Venture —
DSS	= Decision — System	LT	= — Time
P&L	= Profit and —	BAM	= — and Mortar
2Q	= Second —	SBU	= Strategic — Unit
CIO	= Chief — Officer	WIP	= — in Progress
HQ	= Head —	KPI	= Key — Indicators
KM	= — Management	IPO	= Initial — Offer
VA	= — Analysis	PLC	= Public — Company
ASAP	= As — as —	VAT	= Value — Tax

So, what is your score? Don't worry, you need not tell me. But of course, I want you to use it as a pointer for revamping your English upgrade plans to fill in the gaps, or should I say the blanks.

Well these are just some of the common business terms that we come across in the daily workflow. There is a huge sea out there, and the only way to prevent yourself from drowning in it, is by overcoming the 'lost at sea' feeling. And this is possible by hanging onto the lifejacket of constant preparation.

Business acronyms and their nuances in various business contexts make all the difference in the number game. Just as incompatible software programs cause a system crash, similarly, if people are operating on different 'context' platforms, there is bound to be a business crash. Hence, corporations these days, invest in special English courses, which are aimed at not only imparting the language skills, but also focus on developing effective communication skills. That which works well on the tip of the tongue works well in business development too.

Another major aspect of Business English is cultural awareness; it helps professionals to move across cultures with the required level of sensitivity.

6.3 A Seamless Web of Cultures—'Grow Together'

> The English language is a cultural mosaic
> And a confluence of different views,
> Which are two very great virtues.

Just like the Internet is the virtual knowledge capital of the world, English is the virtual cultural capital of the world. Disagreement is a part of life, but to reach an amicable consensus is a bigger part of life. There may be more native speakers of Chinese, but when it comes to communicating across cultures, English is the *first* choice, as it is integral to bringing about cross-cultural sophistication and integration. Trust is vital in all communication and English helps to build it.

We all have our own cultures and we are extremely proud of the same. One of the most effective ways of enriching our culture is by sharing it with others, and also by encouraging positive influences from other cultures to enter into our cultural realms. English is one such language that helps to keep the world heritage alive by blending in all the good aspects of various cultures. Whatever is the binding factor—there are five main points, which we need to keep in mind while building a web of cultures:

- Listen with patience and empathy
- Do not indulge in criticism
- Display an attitude of objectivity, and behavior of openness and cooperation

- Show mutual politeness and respect
- Look for common ground rather than areas of conflict

English as a tool of integration and mass collaboration can be wielded to incorporate these points for building *positive* relationships. We are all peace-loving souls and to strike a fruitful dialog for establishing a common bond, we need to use English. English communication lets you cross cultural barriers and time zones. As a transnational linguistic tool, it gives the opportunity to oppressed communities to raise their issues, mobilize protests and even challenge authorities. English is building new trends and patterns of social cohesion, *continually*.

> **Spotlight**
>
> Self-expression and communication is a human necessity, and English is a global necessity of mankind.
>
> You need to make an effort to integrate with the local people in order to develop your personal communication skills.

Interpersonal communication is the key to building a seamless web of cultures. It is occurring every single minute of the day. For example, a native Hindi (India) speaker, who takes the time to learn English before traveling to Washington, will be in a better position to understand the street signs, menu items, directions, and relate well to the local customs. By making the effort to speak to people in their language, the Indian traveler is showing the willingness to accept a foreign culture without holding any language indifferences. This simple act of trying to express oneself in the other language shows a sense of mutual respect, and this is usually appreciated and reciprocated as well.

English is not just about passing exams or signing a multimillion dollar business contract. It is a tool for building social bonds. To be able to build sensitivity and empathy towards various cultures, interpersonal communication skills are of utmost importance. These bonds of understanding and communication can be created through the sharing of meaningful messages by using a common language, which is English.

A Word of Caution

Many believe English definitely acts as a good binding factor amongst cultures, which adds to the seamless cohesion factor, whereas some factions are of the opinion that English tends to divide people along linguistic lines. But again, we cannot forget that regions and communities are majorly divided along social, political or religious lines.

6.3.1 Cross-cultural Sensitivity—'An integral part and parcel of social life'

The knowledge of English helps to tailor your mannerisms, behavior, and the way you approach cross-cultural communication situations. This in turn will maximize the potential of everyone involved in the process to adapt nicely to each others' cultures.

As English easily fits into any socio-cultural context, it acts as a bonding factor, whereby it links people from different walks of life by constantly reshaping itself to suit the needs of the people. English is one such language that can easily transplant itself on foreign soils thereby enculturing itself to reflect a diversity of disparate cultures. This in a way helps to neutralize hard-core regional factors like caste and creed. As people have their own version of this language for communication purposes, they feel secure, and at the same, also feel connected to the world due to its international appeal. Thus, English builds a multicultural mosaic, as it blends itself in as yet another voice added to the multilingual repertoire of any community.

This goes to show that English and other cultures and languages can coexist. The other languages are definitely important for their local values and culture, whereas English is important for several other special reasons like its ability to link nations and its ability to overlap with local tongues in certain domains. It is important in its own right. These reasons lead to a set of advantages:

- English creates high collectivism, where the focus shifts from personal progress to group progress.
- English instills the habit of examining your own communication patterns and their cross-cultural implications.

- English creates interest in people to participate in community-led initiatives like education, social service, community service, etc.
- English encourages cultural immersion.

English may be an expression for American lifestyle or a status symbol of the elites, but by going beyond this limited perspective, one realizes that English is the common denominator of humanity too. English is needed to handle issues of international relations, world security and peace. It is about adjusting your linguistic behavior to new situations, new people and new roles.

World peace is a burning issue these days. One of the most important factors for establishing dialog between various nations and peace organizations is language, and English plays a major role in establishing empathy and understanding of various views. This understanding is very essential to build respect for difference and nurture cultural tolerance. The Peacekeeping English Project (PEP) managed by the British Council is one major initiative which focuses on peace building and conflict resolution through improved English language communication.

6.4 Tickle Your Brains—'Match-making'

Match the statements on the left hand side in the table with the respective emotions on the right hand side.

Statement	*Emotion*
The apprentice is worried about his blunder	Tense
The old lady enjoys her meditation session	Violent
The little girl is trembling with fear because she has failed in her test	Guilty
Sam beats up his little brother	Relaxed

6.5 Questions for Reflection

1. What parameters do you use to gauge a person's English proficiency level?
2. What do you think is the impact of the growing importance of the marriage between Internet and English?

3. What is your opinion about having English as an official language for the Internet?
4. Why do you think it is important for professionals to specialize in Business English?
5. How does your organization leverage the knowledge of English to adjust your communication patterns with the needs of different corporate cultures?
6. Will the presence of an official global language kill the motivation to learn other languages?
7. Is English just a tool to communicate or has more dimensions to it?

6.6 Chapter Recap

A. English is the most important tie that binds us together on several levels, and builds a broad-minded cultural and linguistic perspective.

B. Research has proved that knowledge of English hones the problem-solving skills, enhances creativity and sharpens the conceptualizing abilities. English is all about building transnational competencies and a seamless learning continuum.

C. Because of a plethora of methods available for learning English, right from online dictionaries to social networking sites, the seamless learning continuum is heading towards convenience and comfort.

D. Correct usage and the context matter a lot, or else a state of confusion is bound to arise. Factors like situational and cultural context need to be considered to break down barriers in the communication cycle.

E. Corporations with a lot of respect for English, not only reap huge profits in their local markets, but are able to forge links with the global corporate culture too.

F. Just as corporate culture and policies influence the level of English skills, in the similar manner, English plays a major role in inculcating proper business ethics and corporate culture.

G. Every industry has its own acronyms and core vocabulary. To survive in your chosen field, you will need to know not only these acronyms in-depth, but also the language in which these acronyms are—English.

H. There may be more native speakers of Chinese, but when it comes to communicating across cultures, English is the *first* choice.

I. Interpersonal communication is the key to building a seamless web of cultures. It is occurring every single minute of the day.

J. The bonds of understanding and communication can be created through the sharing of meaningful messages by using a common language, which is English.

K. English may be an expression for American lifestyle or a status symbol of the elites, but by going beyond this limited perspective, one realizes that English is the common denominator of humanity too. English is needed to handle issues of international relations, world security and peace.

L. World peace is a burning issue these days. One of the most important factors for establishing dialog between various nations and peace organizations is language, and English plays a major role in establishing empathy and understanding of various views. This understanding is very essential to build respect for difference and nurture cultural tolerance.

Importance of English in Various Fields

7

No English = no job offers.
Leap onto the English-speaking bandwagon
And then there will be no more growth blockers.

English is *universally* acknowledged as the language of various fields, right from a tourist guide to a medical transcriptionist. The vast majority of those who achieve global recognition in their respective fields are English-speaking and active contributors to the knowledge society that we all live in.

English is the most widely published language. The global spread of English over the last 35-40 years is remarkable. The rise in cutting-edge online communication has made the business world rethink its strategies, right from risk management to media coverage. And to keep pace with dynamic changes in accessing and creating quality content for all sorts of industries, English is the key driver. These days, most of the industries are web-based and they cannot afford to ignore this driver.

The explosion of the communications technology domain has revolutionized the domain of English language learning and teaching. It has gone beyond the boundaries of academic learning and teaching, and it has adapted itself to accommodate the learning and teaching of more specialized areas, ESP—English for Specific Purposes. ESP covers subjects varying from business management to tourism, to the medical field.

With its dominance in a plethora of industries, English is not only about academic progress and personal growth. With its presence everywhere, it also enhances job prospects. Companies are increasingly hiring professionals who have

English as their forte. They know that people who have successfully finished their course abroad or have spent considerable time in an English-speaking place are likely to possess second language skills—mainly English, knowledge of business practices, and a global mindset. Apart from these attributes, they are also likely to have transnational abilities like understanding of customs, contexts and circumstances, cross-cultural communication skills, behavioral adaptability to situations, analytical skills, team-oriented focus, etc.

No English, no job offers. Look at the job vacancy advertisements in magazines and columns in the newspapers they invariably state 'must be well-versed in the English language'. Whether it is the finance industry, or the hospitality sector, or the IT domain, it is English the employers are asking for.

Tourism, real estate, marketing, media or the medical industry, their main aim is that of sustainable development, and English is the vehicle for this kind of development.

> **Spotlight**
> Any business enterprise that understands the importance of quality content has the best chance to beat others in the competitive race.

These days, several companies request writing samples along with the résumé. This is so true for media-related companies. Why do you think they do so? They are not just interested in what is there on your résumé, but are also interested in knowing whether you can apply it—can you write an effective report or a properly worded advertising tag line. The 'practical value' is what they are trying to verify.

7.1 ESP—'English for Specific Purposes'

English for Specific Purposes is about learning the language for fulfilling special functions, and this learning is structured based on the assessment of needs and purpose of the learners—it is *learner-centered.* The learners focus on the language skills related to their respective subject matter areas, disciplines or specialties. The needs and not the learning policies and methods are the driving factor in imparting linguistic knowledge. If we are to remain focused on supplying the fast-changing, globalized human capital with up-to-date skills, then ESP is the key.

ESP is mainly a result of tireless efforts put in by linguistic pioneers, who believed that developing and enhancing the ways in which a language is used in real communication situations is the real deal. One of the main advantages of ESP is that the learners are able to apply all that they have learned in 'real' life contexts. As the learners find the ESP technique relevant in nature, they are bound to be motivated to grasp this language faster.

There are various types of ESP with absolute and variable characteristics associated with them. This in itself can be a topic for a full-fledged book. Sticking to the objectives of this book, it is useful for us to know that ESP is a needs-driven and purpose-oriented way of learning the English language.

7.2 English and the Age of Internet—'Window to Technology-based Resources'

> To survive the shockwaves of this era,
> English and Internet, this duo
> Is the modern *mantra*.

Before the birth of Internet, it was difficult to learn English, since the only way to acquire fluency in the language was through a costly college degree or a language program. As the Internet originated from the West, English was an inherent part of it. With the rapid spread of Internet, the proliferation of English was a natural outcome. Internet-driven tutoring combines the power of both audio and video inputs to derive the most out of English teaching. The mutual growth of both these mediums can be traced back to the 60s, right from the "Eve" network—Advanced Research Projects Agency Network (ARPANET) to the contemporary global Internet. The rapid surge in the popularity of English is because of the fact that Internet provides free and open access to one and all; there are no censors and restrictions.

Internet is a wealth of English-based resources and a true attestation of this fact is that with the click of a button, you can access as many sites as you wish, all in one go. For example, you could search for website links to English learning resources, and then e-mail these to all your friends in one go. With the advent of online universities and distance education, it has become possible for more people to learn this language.

English as an entity takes on new forms in the age of Internet. Average age of Internet users is in the range 18-40. Almost 1.78 billion people worldwide are Internet-friendly. You must be wondering why all these Internet-related figures? Well, most of the Internet users speak English as native or secondary language. Internet and English is a unique combination of technology and art, and taste and craft.

Latest technological innovations and English are two sides of the same coin. Both together represent a 'Network of networks'. Tim Burners-Lee, credited as the inventor of the World Wide Web, once said that the Internet is "less a technological fact than a social fact and its chief stock-in-trade is language". Just as the importance of Internet is growing rapidly, so is the prominence of English too. Riding on the crest of the Internet revolution, English has consolidated its dominance as the language of the Internet. This hi-tech marriage of the Internet and English has produced an argot of words and idioms.

In 1996, *The Economist* aptly described this language, "English may now be impregnably established as the world standard language: an intrinsic part of the global communications revolution".

The most precious intellectual assets of any organization are its human resources. In order for the human resources to be vigilant and up-to-date, they need to sift through a variety of printed and computer-based sources of information, and most of this information is in English. The knowledge of English is necessary for them so that they can help their organization to capitalize on the current trends in their respective fields. This vigilance can be developed and nurtured with the dual dose of Internet and English. This very tonic benefits and enriches business communities across the globe.

> **Spotlight**
> English integrates people from all over the world on the Internet. This makes Internet a society of free individuals that permeates all spheres of life.

English is that lubricant which adds dynamism to the vehicle of progress and keeps it focused and prevents any mishaps on the information superhighway. In turn, this superhighway provides online courses, online universities that make it possible for more people to learn English. This superhighway provides opportunities to people who may live in countries where access to education facilities is limited or not up to the mark.

English is that engine which gives us understanding of how to deal with new technologies in the future. Apart from the technological revolution and economies of scale, the combination of Internet and English will ultimately result in the establishment of an information society.

The Internet surge is affecting the ways in which we think; it is influencing each and every aspect of our living—education, business, shopping, travel and many more. But most of all, it is creating a revolution in the manner in which we communicate. This intellectual revolution is something that each one of us wants to be a part of. And English is the answer. As the importance of the Internet is growing rapidly, it becomes more and more important to know how to use the various Internet services available, and as a part of this, to speak, read and write English is necessary.

7.2.1 Information and Communications Technology—'English for Specific Purposes'

A postgraduate student needs to learn how to use the Internet for a college thesis, a senior finance manager needs to know how to operate high-level MIS (Management Information Systems) modules for decision-making, an accountant needs to use information technology for executing his tasks, and a housewife needs to log on to an online shopping portal, but to perform all these operations, they need to first have a basic-level education in computers. And even prior to this basic knowledge is the knowledge of English.

In spite of the growth of Internet in several languages, English is the main language of the Internet users, be it for general surfing or an online language course. It is interesting to note that the computing vocabulary of many languages is borrowed from English. An everyday example related to using computers is debugging errors due to software bugs or hardware glitches. It is much more probable that the solution to your problem is posted on one of the many English language technical forums than on one of the few local language ones.

Most of the technological resources come in the form of books, e-books, websites, periodicals, journals, online libraries, podcasts, etc. These resources are mostly available in English. For this reason, scholars frequently refer to its latest phase as *World English*.

Because organizations place so much value on intellectual assets, they are turning to the Internet to maximize this value through online exchanges of these assets. To build this value and enhance performance in an Internet-enabled market, organizations need to integrate the skills of people across borders, and this is where English steps in to leverage the power of these assets to bring about differentiation and value addition to the organizations. Majority of the assets are in English—technical diagrams and illustrations, corporate websites, corporate values, patents, portfolios, training manuals, user guides, discussion groups, technical manuals, technology forums, technical bulletins, etc.

English proficiency equates to Internet proficiency. E-learning indicates more written and spoken learning inputs and that too quickly. The vast resources available on the Internet help learners of English to develop awareness of the cultures and human values across the world, in minimal amount of time.

7.2.2 Learning English on the Internet Worksheet

The Learning English on the Internet worksheet lets you understand your attitudes towards E-learning of English. It also lets you develop a concrete idea of your learning habits and patterns associated with Internet-based learning.

How much percentage of efforts do you put in (on the internet) for improving the various English language skills:

(a) Communication
(b) Networking
(c) Writing
(d) Cross-cultural sensitivity and understanding
(e) Reading
(f) Comprehension
(g) Speaking

How much percentage of your time you spend on Internet for honing your English language aptitude from the following locations:

(a) University/College
(b) Workplace
(c) Home
(d) Computer café
(e) Friend's home
(f) Others

Performance Indicator	Agree	Disagree	Any other observations	Improvement measures
Internet improves the social value of English				
Web-assisted lessons promote the habit of self-study				
Internet enhances the acquisition rate of English				
E-resources in classes create a positive learning atmosphere				
Internet tools (chat rooms, discussion groups, etc.) instill the habit of group learning				
Computer-mediated communication engages people in real-life collaborative communication				

Please list what you consider to be the greatest benefit of Internet resources for learning English?

(Contd...)

Please describe the type of online training you have taken for improving your English skills?

What kind of support teachers can provide in web-based learning?

What is your opinion on using the Internet for learning English (helpful, not required, uninteresting, interesting, not sure)?

Answer the following statements using the options—Yes/No

(a) Learning to use a new Internet service may take a few hours, a few days or even weeks, but it takes years to learn a language

(b) Do you often mix up Internet terminology with business phraseology in your daily workflow

(c) Factors like personality, age, previous knowledge and socio-economic status influence the E-learning experience

7.3 E-Commerce—'A Growing Trend'

E-Commerce and E-nglish
Are two sides of the same story.

The world is becoming smaller and smaller. We all are experiencing this paradigm *byte-by-byte,* on a daily basis. A China-based company acquires raw material from UK to deliver products in Greece, or better still, you buy Taiwan made gadgetry which is programmed by US engineers and you use it in Denmark. These examples are just a snapshot of what we all are experiencing. All these aspects of commerce and now E-Commerce are based on a vast pool of information. And 80 per cent of the information is transmitted, processed and analyzed using English. English is not just a language but also a potential commerce tool. If this tool is used wisely in the e-space, E-Commerce is bound to reap a lot of benefits.

E-Commerce solutions offer minimum overheads, cheaper marketing costs, and a growing global customer base. One of the main factors for these advantages is English. The dynamic role played by English in E-Commerce ventures is changing the marketplace and industry structures, consumer behavior and labor conditions, and products and services. All these dynamic changes create new economic dimensions and opportunities, even in the midst of the global recession.

Many of the E-Commerce products and services are complex in nature, and need robust and on-going customer services. A huge percentage of the Internet-savvy population/end-users uses English. Therefore, in order to address the end-user problems in real-time, English is a must. Moreover, an English-language website is particularly important for the E-Commerce companies as this helps them in reaching out to a wide customer base.

Electronic supply and demand make factors like security and trust all the more important in E-Commerce solutions and transactions. Most of these aspects are dealt with in English, and the lack of knowledge of this language clearly means loopholes in the supporting policies. Thus, English is one of the main factors for capitalizing on the vast E-Commerce potential.

7.4 Media—'Cross National Boundaries'

> The role of English in media
> Is much more than breaking news;
> It is about providing various views.

English and Media have been complementing each other right from the 17th century onwards, but in a limited way due to several restrictions. It is only from the 19th century onwards that the concept of independent press started gaining momentum, and this in turn was propelled by modern printing technology.

From the turn of the 19th century, multinational companies began to operate on a global scale by leveraging the power of latest technologies, which resulted in the explosion of large scale marketing and advertising options. English has always played and still plays a central role in fuelling this explosion further. What has kept this trend going is the fact that this explosion, to a greater or lesser extent, has affected each and every nation in the world.

Any media option also needs to show sensitivity and social responsibility towards society and its issues. These days, as everything is going global, so has the media industry. Keeping in line with global needs, English is a must. They are several points to this: Media and English go hand-in-hand—

(a) They are mediums that let us not only to mine the experiences and knowledge of the world-wide community but also to connect with it to enhance our understanding of the global experiences.

(b) They report the happenings all over the world in clear terms. The rate of errors of omission and commission goes down thereby increasing coverage on news.

(c) They are all-pervasive. Whether it is a radio broadcast or a newspapers article or a television program, the target audiences are interested in not just local happenings, but also in worldwide news.

(d) They influence each and every aspect of the symbolic space that we operate in, which in turn shapes our existence, decisions and identity.

Proficiency in English in the media professionals gives the audiences a better chance to understand the news and share their objective feedback to influence the modalities that affect the various spheres of their lives. These points lead to a transparent interaction between media and the audiences thereby increasing the credibility of the news and the media professionals. Finally, it is about marketing identities in one form or the other through this language.

7.4.1 Advertising—'Global appeal, international flavor'

By the turn of the 19th century, advertising in English became a big competitive industry in itself. So much so that glossy magazines and newspaper supplements totally dedicated to advertisements mushroomed in all parts of the world. Mass production and mass consumption made this possible.

Apart from the target group and differentiation factors, advertising is also about communicating key messages, which in turn convinces end-users to buy the products/services and remain loyal to these products/services. Communication, persuasion and influencing the mindset are nothing but a language game. Viewers view products/services endorsed in English as having a global appeal, an international flavor of sophistication.

One may think that the company's logo and tagline is its true salesman. And this thought is absolutely correct, but what makes this possible is the strong medium of language and English is that medium to achieve a mass reach.

These days, mere black and white content does not hold a customer's attention for too long. What gets accurate feedback to the companies for their products and services are interactive advertising options like the Internet, audio visuals and multimedia. What gets companies big figures is a lucrative advertising strategy designed to influence the purchasing behavior or thought patterns. With English taking center stage in the online advertising world, companies need to ensure that their advertising teams are strong in it.

The right combination of advertising medium and catchy punch lines is what makes a product or service stand out against the backdrop of stiff competition. Research statistics indicate companies that adopt a well-thought out English-driven interactive advertising campaign are the ones to break even and achieve outstanding sales figures.

Clever companies know their languages well. They make use of local English versions combined with certain foreign words to create an impressive advertising campaign. One such example that comes to my mind is the punch line of "Hungry Kya?" ('Are you hungry?' in English), a healthy concoction of English and Hindi (Hinglish) found in an advertisement for Domino's Pizza in India. This kind of a text structure can be termed as 'Globalized, persuasive, impressive brand building', and this is the *mantra* for achieving success in cross-border marketing strategies. Even in the multinational marketing scenarios, the hybrid approach gives preference to using English more than any other language, in combination with the vernacular medium.

Today, advertisement is not just about conveying punch lines, it goes beyond this. At the end of the day, it is about reaching the goal of aggressive sales promotion, and this is where English steps in. English being a reflection of multiple voices, not only appeals to a wider audience, but also helps to create a favorable impression about the products and services.

I am sure many of you must have had the following experience on your business trips to non-native English speaking countries. For example, you are watching television in your hotel room in Korea. There will advertisements that are shown both in English and then the regional language. There you go! This proves the importance of English yet again. This trend of bilingual marketing is very popular in countries where English is not the first or official language.

These days, major companies leverage the power of social networking sites, again combining this power with the enormous symbolic value of English works wonders. They believe this kind of advertising to be a part of the larger social media strategy, which serves two main purposes: (1) *Instant* connection with the customers (2) *Instant* customer feedback and customer insights. Such social outlets of advertising help in communication, collaboration and community building with the customer base.

7.4.2 Press—'Wide reach and up-to-date'

International news is broadcasted in English; major names include news networks such as British Broadcasting Corporation (BBC), National Broadcasting Company (NBC) and Cable News Network (CNN). There is a reason for this kind of English usage and reach. As it is the main language of communication, these news channels understand its implication and use it to broadcast everything under the sun, right from grassroots happenings to up-to-date news. This also goes to show that English news reach faster and are more updated than local news channels.

Similarly, international syndicates of magazines, journals and newspapers are in English. More than half of the newspapers published in the world are in English.

What is interesting to note about English is that it is not about how and where it is used, rather the sole quality of 'being the most noticeable' works wonders for all sorts of press occasions.

Internet has also played a major role in strengthening the foothold of English in the press. As it is quickly becoming a new mass medium, Internet is an imperative tool for the reporters and journalists community to possess in order to operate effectively in the online-press world. With the prolific growth of

English-based content on the Internet, we will need more and better educated reporters and journalists to extract, present and publish the relevant bits of information from the large mass of grapevine doing the rounds in the cyberspace circuit.

Even in countries like India, impact of English as a linguistic tool is great. English-language newspapers are published in practically all states of India, which provide a diversity of viewpoints on various factors.

7.4.3 Marketing—'English is the perfect pitch'

As international markets are flourishing at a rapid pace, so are marketing strategies to tap these markets.

You may be a salesperson on the move in India or a vice-president of sales of a multinational firm in the United States. What is that one aspect which keeps you ahead of your counterparts? Do I hear echoes of 'Marketing Pitch' skittering across in the background? Bingo! Marketing is the focal point of all organizations.

The true competitive advantage of companies is making their presence felt globally and English plays a central role in this. Be it a billboard, or a neon sign, or a commercial on a channel, or a poster, you will find English 'glowing' on it. English gives the companies the *power of presence*, both physically and virtually.

Promotional material is all in English. Is this an overstatement? Let's discuss it in this section. With path-breaking online marketing services, it is imperative for companies to design marketing strategies and materials that will create an environment of interactive marketing. Given the number of English speakers all over the world and online content which is mainly English-driven, this language plays a significant role in helping the marketing departments of companies to exercise their power of persuasion.

Companies use English as a means of marketing not only for producing favorable impact on their consumers, but they too feel with English, they can give their brand a cosmopolitan and modern identity. Companies also use language as a means of strengthening social identity. For gaining a greater reach, they need to combine the symbolistic status of English with tailor-made campaigns to attract various demographic groups. This is the reason why so many big brands like Pepsi, Mars and Cadburys have become household names today.

7.5 Medical—'Tailor-made Care'

English and person-centered Medicare
Shatter a patient's nightmare.

The role of the medical industry goes far beyond saving the lives of people rather this industry is one of the most critical community resources. When it is a matter of life and death, communication glitches are not at all permissible. English is important not only for building a patient-centered approach and enabling a great professional-patient interaction, but also within the healthcare team and inter-hospital communication. The central focus is on providing the necessary therapeutic procedures and services without any vicarious delays.

With the enormous influx of foreign tourists in several countries, it is necessary for the medical professionals to have a good grip over the English language to meet the communication needs of an increasingly diverse patient base and provide accurate patient care. A smooth exchange of information between the healthcare providers and patients ensures that there is no misdiagnosis, wrong treatment administered or unnecessary wastage of time, money and efforts in incorrect tests. It also allows patients to share their concerns with the healthcare staff.

Recently, the nursing council has increased the IELTS band score from 6.5 to 7 to ensure that nurses act as an error-free communication link between doctors and patients.

The practices and their related documents—laboratory tests and expert diagnosis reports, medical software and user manuals, patient information leaflets and registration details, and patents need to be highly meticulous and error-free, for which full grasp of medical terminology is absolutely essential. This is where English steps in.

For advancement in career, doctors and medical professionals need to take part in medical conferences held in English and contribute articles in English to international journals, so that their work gets wider exposure and acceptance.

There is a growing presence of in-house communication centers to handle all aspects related to communication. These centers help both the ends—medical staff and patients to participate effectively in the clinical decision-making process. Private and public medical organizations have developed interpreter certification programs that are designed for full-time professional interpreters. This is necessary where professionals have to deal with both native and non-native patients. English is the key to 'healthy' healthcare delivery services and practices.

7.6 Travel and Tourism—'At Your Service'

> If you are going international,
> Then English cannot be optional.

Over the years, international travel has increased by leaps and bounds. The reasons for traveling across boundaries are many and various. This trend has led to an increase in investment in as well as returns from the Tourism sector. Right from parallel menus to street signs, English is used in conjunction with local languages.

All of us are travelers on countless occasions throughout our lives, and international travelers find that speaking English can make their travels a lot easier and hassle-free. This makes their experiences much more fluid in nature, which in a way, helps them to cut across the borders of caste, age, gender, ethnicity and language.

Local tourism boards need to step up and play a major role in ensuring that their tourism policies are not only focused at making money, but also focus on providing a comfortable experience to the visitors through promotion, attraction development, and of course a support system for English in place. Only then English-speaking tourists will get their value for money.

Most of the communication material related to the tourism and travel industry is designed in English. Brochures, tour guides, travel websites, tour instructions, menus, directions, audio and visual aids. Whether it is emergency instructions in a hotel or safety instructions on international flights, English is used invariably. Apart from these aspects, English is a must for handling activities related to hospitality management and customer services (handling customer relations, handling telephone calls, answering questions, sharing the relevant information).

> **Spotlight**
> On my first visit to Malaysia, I had some friends who visited me. They had brought along with them CDs of some of the most popular plays. I was wondering as to how I was going to understand any of this. But to my surprise, the theater had a provision to sell bilingual programs with the summaries and subtitles of the plays in both English and Malay. Now, isn't that creative!

Travel agents are the ones who deal with all sorts of travelers. In fact, they are the first point of contact for any international traveler. For offering the most suitable advice on destinations and making arrangements for visa, transportation, hotel accommodations, etc., the travel agents need to be well-versed in English.

7.6.1 Lesson 6—'Travel directions need to be properly worded'

Illustration 7.1: Improperly Worded Directions can Cause Mishaps

The old lady is all aghast after reading the accident-prone instructions. They have such a deep impact on her that she actually visualizes the scene, in case she was to really follow these deadly instructions (blindly). I can imagine her mental plight.

Accidents often occur because of poor communication and these are amplified due to other factors like lack of awareness, language barriers, lack of training, etc.

7.7 Exercise—'Food for Thought'

It is time for some mental action. Choose the correct option.

1. One of the most important aims of a marketing strategy __ expansion of the customer base.

   Options: (A) are (B) is (C) Both A and B

2. Our new marketing plan is showing increased__.

   Options: (A) profits (B) profitably (C) None

3. We just __ two new contracts from our most esteemed client.

   Options: (A) got (B) brought (C) A or B (D) landed

4. The management __ the marketing proposal.

   Options: (A) is approved (B) just has approved (C) None (D) has just approved

7.8 Questions for Reflection

1. How can feedback and professional learning experience (using English) be consolidated to improve profitability in various service industries like media and tourism?
2. What kind of social media marketing tools do you use to reach out to the English-speaking customers?
3. Do you think English can keep up with the future speed of information density?
4. Why do you think the learner-centered approach is an effective approach of learning languages?
5. What effects do the New Englishes have on fields like marketing, tourism, etc.?

6. How do instances of communicative competence (using English) contribute to business?
7. How do you leverage your knowledge of English for adding value to your company's products and services?
8. Describe the challenges your company faces while trying to tap the power of English for its products/ services?
9. What policies has your company adopted to ensure that English acquisition scales up to the business needs?

7.9 Chapter Recap

A. Latest technological innovations and English are two sides of the same coin.

B. English is that lubricant which adds dynamism to the vehicle of progress and keeps it focused and prevents any mishaps on the information superhighway.

C. In spite of the growth of Internet in several languages, English is the main language of the Internet users. It is interesting to note that the computing vocabulary of many languages is borrowed from English.

D. Many of the E-Commerce products and services are complex in nature, and need robust and on-going customer services. In order to address the end-user problems in real-time, English is a must.

E. Apart from the technological revolution and economies of scale, the combination of Internet and English will ultimately result in the establishment of an information society.

F. The explosion of the communications technology domain has revolutionized the domain of English language learning and teaching. It has gone beyond the boundaries of academic learning and teaching, and it has adapted itself to accommodate the learning and teaching of more specialized areas (ESP—English for Specific Purposes). ESP covers subjects varying from business management to tourism.

G. Tourism, marketing, media or the medical industry, their main aim is that of sustainable development, and English is the vehicle for effectuating this kind of development.

H. One may think that the company's logo and tagline is its true salesman. And this thought is absolutely correct, but what makes this possible is the strong medium of language, and English is that medium to achieve a mass reach.

I. International syndicates of newspapers, magazines and journals are in English. More than half of the newspapers published in the world are in English.

J. Viewers view products/services endorsed in English as having a global appeal, an international flavor of sophistication.

K. Most of the communication material related to the tourism and travel industry is designed in English.

L. The true competitive advantage of companies is making their presence felt globally and English plays a central role in this. Be it a billboard, or a neon sign, or a commercial on a channel, or a poster, you will find English 'glowing' on it. English gives the companies the *power of presence*, both physically and virtually.

M. English is important not only for building a patient-centered approach and enabling a great professional-patient interaction, but also within the healthcare team and inter-hospital communication. The central focus is on providing the necessary therapeutic procedures and services without any vicarious delays.

PART-III

From Learners to Performers

How to Improve English—'Basics Matter A Lot'

8

In the earlier sections, we discussed the what, where, when and why of the English language. In this chapter, we will deal with *how* to improve the English language skills.

Grammar is a set of rules inherent to any language, which help to gain knowledge of *how* a language works. While there are hundreds of rules of grammar in the English language, there are certain rules that are an absolute necessity. The more we are aware of Grammar dynamics—the rules of structure and the rules to transform the structure, the more we can polish our use of the language.

English is an Analytic language. Instead of depending on word endings, English uses grammatical rules and conventions to establish meaning and relationships.

8.1 Basic Sentence Structure—'The Building Blocks'

A sentence is a collection of words that gives it a coherent meaning. Subject, object and predicate are the basic building blocks of a sentence. Let us discuss these blocks:

A. **Subject:** The subject is usually a noun. It is used to identify a person, place, quality or thing. It usually answers the question who/what is the sentence about?

B. **Object:** The object receives the action and usually follows the verb.

C. **Predicate:** The predicate contains the verb. The verb usually follows the subject and describes a particular action, event or a state of being.

D. There are two types of clauses used in sentences—independent and dependent. Independent clauses have a subject and verb, and are complete sentences which express a concrete thought or idea. Dependent clauses also have a subject and verb, but they do not express a complete thought. A dependent clause has a dependent marker (after, though, despite, etc.). These two types can be used in a number of ways to form the four basic types of sentences.

Examples:

Jane and Jess enjoy fabric painting.

Although Jane and Jess enjoy fabric painting....

Looking at the sentences, one can instantly conclude that the first sentence is an independent clause and can stand alone, whereas the second one is not complete and is a dependent clause.

8.1.1 Types of Sentences—'From Simple to Compound-complex'

Based on the number of clauses in a sentence, it can be categorized into one of the following types:

A. **Simple Sentence:** It contains a single subject and predicate to describe one idea. Both the subject and predicate can be either a single word or a set of words.

Example 1: Girls sing (subject and predicate are single words).

Example 2: The cash flow software module needs a lot of rework (subject and predicate are a set of words).

B. **Compound Sentence:** It is a combination of two or more simple sentences (main clauses) that are joined using a conjunction—for, and, nor, but, or, yet, so. It can also have one or more subordinate clauses.

Example: Jane is fond of drawing, and she attends drawing workshops regularly (two main clauses coupled together).

C. **Complex Sentence:** Complex sentences contain a dependent clause and at least one independent clause.

The two clauses are connected by a subordinator—who, which, if, etc.

Example: That's the girl who topped the mathematics exam.

D. **Compound-Complex Sentence:** These sentences contain at least one dependent clause and more than one independent clause. These clauses are connected by both subordinators and conjunctions.

Example: Greg, who is the chairman of the committee, convened the annual meeting, and his project proposal was well received.

Table 8.1: Recap of the Sentence Types

Recap of the Sentence Types
1. A simple sentence has one independent clause. There is no punctuation to separate the elements.
2. A compound sentence has two independent clauses joined in the following ways: Conjunction (for, and, nor, but, or, yet, so) Semicolon (;) Conjunctive adverb (likewise, therefore, etc.) Punctuation patterns: Independent clause, coordinating conjunction independent clause. Independent clause; independent clause. Independent clause; conjunctive adverb, independent clause.
3. A complex sentence has one dependent clause and at least one independent clause. They are joined in the following ways: Punctuation patterns: Dependent clause, independent clause. Independent clause dependent clause. (no commas, no semicolons) Independent, nonessential dependent clause, clause. Independent essential dependent clause clause. (no commas, no semicolons)

8.1.2 Word Order—'SVO and more'

Word order is very important in English. There are simple rules to follow in order to get your sentences in place:

A. In a simple sentence, the subject (s) comes directly before the verb (v), and the object (o) comes directly after it. It follows the SVO word order.

   Example: The girl (s) eats (v) biscuits (o).

B. At times, a sentence may have a subject that combines a noun/pronoun with a descriptive phrase (s). The remaining portion of the sentence is called the predicate (p).

   Example: People with a high accuracy level (s) need not worry (p).

C. There are certain other elements like adverbs, adverb phrases and indirect objects that are a part of sentences.

   Adverbs or adverb phrases (a) can be found in three places:

   Before the subject, for example, Today (today is the adverb) I have an important seminar to attend.

   After the object, for example, The old lady told stories in a quiet voice ('in a quiet voice' modifies 'told stories' and therefore it is adverbial).

   In the middle of the verb group, for example, The children have already (already is the adverb) completed their school homework.

D. In standard sentences, the subject-verb-object order is followed religiously. Of course, this rule too comes with certain exceptions like indirect objects without to, for example, He often gives her a lift home. In such cases, the indirect object comes in front of the direct object.

8.1.3 Types of Tenses—'No need to get tense'

There are three types of tenses in English—Simple tenses, Continuous tenses and Perfect tenses. Time can be categorized in three parts—The Past (what you did), the Present (what you are doing) and the Future (what you are going to do). Each type of tense has these three parts. The table 8.2 recaps the tenses along with examples.

Table 8.2: English Tenses at a Glance

Simple Past	Simple Present	Simple Future
[VERB + ed] or irregular verbs (saw, began, etc.)	[VERB] + s/es in third person	[will + verb] [am/is/are + going to + verb]
Examples:	*Examples*:	*Examples*:
He **cleared** the exam yesterday.	They **meet** every Saturday.	He **will arrive** tomorrow.
They **made** it to the finals yesterday.	She usually **paints** on Sundays.	She **is going to arrive** tomorrow.
Past Continuous	**Present Continuous**	**Future Continuous**
[was/were + present participle]	[am/is/are + present participle]	[will be + present participle] [am/is/are + going to be + present participle]
Examples:	*Examples*:	*Examples*:
They **were sleeping** when the doorbell rang.	They **are playing** football.	She **will be attending** the seminar tomorrow.
I **was working** in my study room.	I **am writing** now.	They **are going to be attending the** English workshop tomorrow.
Past Perfect	**Present Perfect**	**Future Perfect**
[had + past participle]	[has/have + past participle]	[will have + past participle]
Examples:	*Examples*:	*Examples*:
She **had been** to India several times.	I **have seen** the Eiffel Tower.	You **will have perfected** your English by the time you finish the book.
I **had finished** my motivational seminar.	The children **have finished** their homework.	They **will have finished** the meeting by 11 a.m.

8.2 Conversion of Sentences—'Simple Rules'

Now that we know the various types of sentences, let us discuss how transformation of sentences takes place.

A. **Conversion of Simple sentences into Compound sentences.** A simple sentence can be converted into a compound sentence by expanding a word or a phrase into a clause and by using the coordinating conjunction (and, but, etc.) to connect the clauses.

Example: Besides being a consultant, she is a writer. (Simple sentence)

She is not only a consultant but also a writer. (Compound sentence)

B. **Conversion of Compound sentences into Simple sentences.** A simple rule to remember for this conversion is reducing the number of clauses to one. You can do so by using prepositional (beside, along, by, for, etc.), participial or infinitive phrases (to + base form of the verb—to eat, to run, etc.).

Example: You must arrive on time, or you cannot attend the meeting. (Compound sentence)

You must arrive on time in order to attend the meeting. (Simple sentence)

In the example, the clause 'or you cannot attend the meeting' is replaced by the infinitive phrase 'in order to attend the meeting'.

C. **Conversion of Simple sentences into Complex sentences.** A simple sentence can be transformed into a complex sentence by expanding a word or phrase into a subordinate clause. This expansion can be achieved using an adjective clause, an adverb clause or a noun clause.

Example of adjective clause:

A good book always teaches you something new. (Simple sentence)

A book that is good always teaches you something new. (Complex sentence)

Example of adverb clause:

He was too tired to continue his exercise regime. (Simple sentence)

He was so tired that he could not continue his exercise regime. (Complex sentence)

Example of noun clause:

She liked her sister's recommendation. (Simple sentence)

She liked what her sister recommended. (Complex sentence)

D. **Conversion of Complex sentences into Simple sentences.** Split your sentences at connection points. These splits result in breaking the clauses apart and you get separate simple sentences.

Example: Patience is a virtue because it lets you overcome obstacles. (Complex sentence)

Patience is a virtue. It lets you overcome obstacles. (Simple sentence)

E. **Conversion of Affirmatives into Negatives.** A Positive sentence tells us what someone/something is, has or does. A Negative sentence means exactly the opposite and 'not' is used in the sentence.

Example: Positive—She will come.
Negative—She will not come.

F. **Conversion from Active to Passive voice.** Active voice emphasizes the doer and the subject is the agent of the verb. Passive voice deals with what is happening and the subject is the target of the action. A sentence can be written in either active voice or passive voice without changing its meaning.

Example of active voice: Helen plays the piano.

Example of passive voice: The plants are watered by Mala.

Rules for conversion from active voice to passive voice are as follows:

Change the object of the active voice into the subject of the passive voice.

The main verb in the active voice is changed to a passive verb—"be" + main verb's past participle.

The subject of the active voice is either converted into a prepositional phrase or omitted altogether in the passive voice.

G. **Conversion from Interrogative sentences into Assertive sentences.** An interrogative sentence asks a question. An assertive sentence simply makes a statement. Remove the question mark and change the word order so that an interrogative sentence transforms into an assertive sentence.

Example: Did I ever ask you to do it? (Interrogative)

I never asked you to do it. (Assertive)

8.2.1 Useful Lists—'Keep them handy'

The following lists will help you to apply the rules of conversion with ease. Always keep them handy while solving English exercises.

A. A list of Coordinating Conjunctions

There are 7 coordinating conjunctions. There is an easy way to remember them with the help of an acronym—FANBOYS

F	A	N	B	O	Y	S
For	And	Nor	But	Or	Yet	So

B. A list of Dependent Markers

where, wherever (relating to place)

as, after, before, until, once, since, while, when, whenever (relating to time)

who, which, that (relative pronouns)

although, though, despite

if, even if, even though, how, unless, whether

because, in order to, why

C. A list of Prepositions

about	for	under
above	from	underneath
across	in	until
after	inside	up
against	into	upon
along	like	with
among	near	within
around	off	without
at	of	
before	on	
behind	onto	

(Contd...)

below	out	
beneath	outside	
beside	over	
between	past	
beyond	since	
but	through	
by	throughout	
despite	till	
down	to	
except	toward	

D. A list of Independent Markers

therefore, moreover, thus, consequently, however, since

8.3 How to Avoid Common Errors—'The Dos and Don'ts'

Confused between affect and effect? Are you faced with the it's vs. its syndrome? Knowing and avoiding common mistakes in English is a wise thing to do.

> **Spotlight**
>
> Others may "write right" but you need to "write correctly".
>
> With so many options of getting your literary works, writings and articles published, it is always wise to "write correctly".
>
> Glaring grammatical errors guarantee dramatic disasters!

Believe it or not, there are common grammatical mistakes made by lots of people. Here are quick tips and tricks that you can use to prevent common errors from marring your English usage:

A. When writing, always look things up. Whenever you are not sure how to use a particular word, look it up in a dictionary to find examples of its usage. It is always better to use simple sentences instead of complex sentences. Proofread everything at least once. Seek a second opinion to ensure that all the errors are eliminated.

B. While writing a story or an article, it is quite possible that we teleport forward and back in time. This shifting in tenses is acceptable only if it is meant to show a transition. When you are writing in a particular tense, stick with it.

C. Capitalize the following: The first word of every sentence, the first and important words in a heading or title, proper nouns like names of people, locations, religions, etc., and the first-person singular pronoun, *I*. There are certain exceptions to this rule, when a person's title or post appears after the name, we do not capitalize or even when we use words as modifiers.

D. Comma splices: If you are using a relative clause to identify the person or thing you are talking about, you should not separate it from the main clause with a comma. A comma splice is the use of a comma between two independent clauses. You can usually fix the error by changing the comma to a period and therefore making the two clauses into two separate sentences, or by changing the comma to a semicolon, or by making one clause dependent by inserting a dependent marker word in front of it.

   Incorrect usage: She enjoys playing badminton, it is a great game.

   Correct usage 1 (period): She enjoys playing badminton. It is a great game.

   Correct usage 2 (semicolon): She enjoys playing badminton; it is a great game.

   Correct usage 3 (dependent marker): She enjoys playing badminton as it is a great game.

E. Misuse of punctuation marks (!)—As a general rule, only one punctuation mark should be used to highlight a word/sentence. The exclamation point is used to convey an emphatic declaration, a strong command or a rhetorical question. It is best not to overuse punctuation marks in business communication. An overdose completely destroys the meaning and coherency of a sentence. For example, Great work!!

You deserve all the credit!! Hard work pays! Doesn't this sentence sound overly exclamatory!!!

F. Use of incorrect articles is another common mistake. For example, incorrect usage: An girl sings, correct usage: A girl sings. Remember, using a or an depends on the sound that begins the next word—**a** + singular noun beginning with a consonant and **an** + singular noun beginning with a vowel. English has two types of articles: definite (the) and indefinite (a, an). **A** and **an** are used before nouns that introduce something or someone you have not mentioned before. **The** refers to a particular person/thing.

G. Conjugation of verbs is another area of concern. For example, with the verb 'go'—the conjugation is: go in the present tense, went in the past tense and gone in the past participle. One way of understanding the conjugation of verbs is preparing a chart along with meaningful examples.

H. The number/amount game: Here is an easy chart to guide you:

Number	Amount
Few	Little
Fewer	Less
Many	Much

Amount deals with quantities of things and number deals with the count.

Example 1: Drinking too much beer is injurious to health. This sentence is amount-driven, but it can be expressed with a numeric count too.

Example 2: Drinking too many glasses of beer is injurious to health.

I. When it comes to comparisons, the battle between me and I is an ongoing one. For example, incorrect usage: She is taller than me, correct usage: She is taller than I am. The trick to avoid this error is to remember that the portion after than always has two words—*I am, she is, they are.*

J. Plural forms play havoc with the language. For example, stop giving me advices. Sounds familiar? The phrase "a piece of advice" will help you to remember that it is advice and not advices. Another important tip to follow is that there is no plural form of articles in English.

K. Commonly confused words like lose and loose are often used interchangeably. Though they sound similar in tone, they are absolutely different in meaning. Simple tips like associating the spelling with the meaning can work wonders. Loose means not rigid or tight or restrained, and lose means to be deprived of control, to fail, etc. You can remember this difference by associating the extra o in loose with more room or more space and hence not fixed or contained.

L. I study allot or I study a lot. It is always two words "a lot". Allot means to assign or distribute. One easy tip to remember the difference is that a lot = 2 words = very much.

M. It's vs. its is an ongoing war. The best way to end this war is to remember a simple equation—it's = is a contraction of two words—"it" and "is" or "it" and "has"—so it requires the use of an apostrophe. Its is the possessive form, possession implies ownership, which essentially means something close to us; hence there are no breaks in the word its—one continuous word. Another way of verifying the usage is putting both words in a sentence, in the case of it's, use the expanded form in the sentence. For example, "The cat drank milk from its milk bowl" or "The cat drank milk from it is milk bowl". Need I tell you the correct version? There you go, you already know the usage.

N. Double negatives are considered to be colloquial in tone. Not indicates negation. In formal speech and writing, two negatives cancel each other out and thus produce the affirmative. In formal settings, the following statement "She is not an underperformer in studies" means she is good at academics. In informal speech or writing, "She ain't got no high academic performance" simply means she is an underperformer.

O. Another common mistake is the use of "your" and "you're." Your/you're—your is a possessive pronoun, for example, this is your bag, and you're is a contraction of two words "you" and "are", for example, "you're very good at singing". Your is the possessive form, possession implies ownership, which essentially means something close to us; hence there are no breaks in the word your—it is one continuous word. Another way of verifying the usage is putting both words in a sentence, in the case of you're, use the expanded form in the sentence. For example, "Your bag is expensive" and "You are bag is expensive". The second sentence does not make any sense.

P. "One of my friends got back from London".

   Why friends—plural form? The sentence indicates that you have many friends who are in London, but you are referring to only one of these friends.

Q. American English uses -ize whereas British English uses -ise in words like criticize/criticise. British English retains the letter u in words like colour and flavour, whereas American English omits u. Both are correct, provided you are consistent in their usage throughout your writing.

R. Time matters! In the morning, in the afternoon and in the evening all denote a general time. For a specific time, such as noon and night, you need to use *at*. For example, I prefer studying *at* midnight.

S. The war between two homophones—To vs. Too. Homophones are words that are spelled differently but sound alike. Their meaning and usage is different too. To is used as a preposition (to the theater) or as an infinitive (to write), whereas too means also (She would like to join us too) and it is even used to denote something as excessive (That watch is too expensive). And the word two is the written form for the number 2, and it indicates quantity (I have two laptops).

8.4 How to Improve Written and Spoken English—'Expand Your Options'

Written English and Spoken English are major forms of communication. English is no longer a library language; it is essentially a global social affair. The better your writing and speaking skills are, the more effectively you communicate your point. Many people agree that being a voracious reader is a key to being a good writer and a great speaker. As English is a multicultural tongue, you need to have a sharp awareness of the various communication contexts, both written and spoken.

Developing written and spoken English skills can seem daunting. There are several techniques to improve these skills. When used in combination, they can facilitate rapid improvement. Written and Spoken English is a reflection of your social competence and professional success.

> **Spotlight**
> Carry something English on you—CD, book, newspaper, journal, a deck of flashcards or magazine, you never know when you might have a break to learn new words.

Tips and tricks to enhance your writing skills:

A. Books are your best friend. Select reading material that offers you meaningful, relevant and interesting information; something that you can apply in your written communication too. Reading does not merely pertain to a physical, visual activity. In fact, reading serves a dual purpose. It enhances your writing skills and cognitive skills. There is a whole lot of mental activity happening while reading. Understanding the implicit and explicit meaning, inferring the conceptual meaning, identifying the main theme and sub-themes, scanning for and extracting points of relevance are all cognitive tasks. Reading is a receptive skill, and its application is writing, which is a productive skill—dual advantage.

B. Always start with what you know best. Your ideas may not be in order. It is important that you write on a daily basis. Don't let a blank paper defeat you. After writing for some time, step back and relax. Let your mind wander for a while and then come back to the writing activity. You will have more thoughts to add to the paper.

C. Cut the clutter in your writing. Eliminate unnecessary words or phrases, for example, join (together) or revert (back), the words in brackets are redundant.

D. Always proofread your text. In the subsequent drafts, look for long phrases and convert them into short phrases. Also don't overuse modifiers like very much, really, etc.

E. Sometimes copying a short passage from a book also helps to improve our writing skills. It also lets us develop the habit of interpreting information as we read and reproduce it. The next step of this exercise is of having the same passage with blanks in it and filling in these blanks. The final stage is that of reading the passage and reproducing it in your words.

F. To develop metaphors, there is a very simple exercise. On one side of the page, list down tangible nouns—mountain, stream, etc., and on the right hand side, list down intangible nouns—admiration, beauty, respect, etc. Now combine them in phrases, you will be surprised to see some really novel metaphors.

G. Effective writing is about getting to the point. Often the simplest word/expression can get you full marks and all ears.

H. Avoid using slang words like thing, stuff, etc. They tend to reflect a poor image of your writing proficiency. Replace these vague words with more specific words.

I. Write, write and write. You can either maintain a personal diary, blog or a journal. You can continue to polish your skills by writing essays, contributing articles to newspapers, etc. Moreover, these options also help you to analyze your thoughts, share your experiences with others and improve your writing style.

J. Interesting pictures in newspapers or magazines can prove to be a major booster to get the ink flowing out of your creative quill. Select an interesting image and observe it for a few minutes, and then write about it for the next 10-15 minutes. Try and answer all the aspects—why, what, who when, where and how. This exercise not only builds your written skills, but also sharpens your analytical skills.

Many times we are put into "think on your feet" situations, where the spoken word could get you a great job or help you to strike a big business deal. Tips and tricks to enhance oral proficiency:

A. Do not rush while speaking. Speaking at a reasonable pace allows you to follow correct intonation and rhythm. In-depth knowledge of phonetics, tone, stress and pitch is necessary for producing correct pronunciation patterns. Advanced software can help you to use correct word accentuation and intonation patterns.

B. Pinpoint words that you find difficult to pronounce. Practice them in isolation. You can also practice by conversing with a native speaker or by looking up a dictionary or by downloading pronunciation software.

C. Pick up a paragraph from a book or news article from a newspaper and try paraphrasing it in your own words.

D. Practice reading out aloud and doing so in front of a mirror becomes an added advantage. It helps you to build up your confidence level too.

E. Listen to well-established radio programs and broadcasts. These types of listening inputs help you to learn pronunciation. They also help you to improve your comprehension skills.

F. Listen to your favorite audio books. This activity helps to improve the intonation.

G. Join a language school where accent development coaches help to develop your pronunciation.

H. Record yourself and replay your voice. This is an effective technique for identifying pronunciation mistakes.

I. Having someone with you who knows the language well is extremely helpful since you will receive instant and constructive feedback. A proficient native English practice partner is a definite plus point as he can help you learn the correct pitch fluctuation to express meanings and contextual significance.

J. Try to keep your sentences short and to the point. With short sentences, mental rehearsal also becomes doable. Before speaking always try to plan the sentence formation in your head. Think twice before you open your mouth. Respond to others with insight and terseness.

The bottom line is that to attain high level communicative competencies, you need conscious and constant hard work.

8.5 How to Build Vocabulary—'Get Started Today!'

To sprinkle new life into your English language skills, add new words to your words vault everyday. A well-developed word bank not only gives you the confidence to communicate effectively at work, study, conferences, events, etc., but also creates credibility in the eyes of the target audience. Your word power shapes people's opinion of you.

Living in a borderless society and with the kind of international mobility that we all enjoy, we need to keep ourselves abreast of new happenings and inventions. New happenings and new inventions mean new words, and in order to be an academically well-rounded person, verbal ability needs to be improved.

Spotlight

Increasing vocabulary is not just about word count; it is about using your word power in your day-to-day communication flow, *appropriately*.

Non-native speakers of English, especially students who want to go abroad for higher education, need to clear the Test of English as a Foreign Language (TOEFL) and having a great vocabulary is a plus for clearing this exam.

A Word of Caution

The kind of vocabulary you use should always be appropriate to the context.

Using bombastic, flowery words without substance will serve no purpose.

Here are a number of techniques to expand your vocabulary:

A. Reading is one of the best ways to improve vocabulary. Be it fiction or non-fiction, or magazines or journals, you are bound to come across new words. Keep a pocket dictionary at hand so that you understand the contextual meaning of the new words. Reading aloud is more effective as it improves comprehension.

B. Join a well-resourced library. Such libraries organize reading sessions, which help you to re-establish a connection with quality reading through a wealth of quality books. In fact, you get to learn more in such a peer-supported environment.

C. Maintain a vocabulary diary and keep it close at hand so that you can jot down new words in it. Adding your own definitions in simple terms helps to remember new words better.

D. Use mnemonics methods like pegging, keywords, rhymes and word associations. Associate pleasant thoughts and images with words. The saying 'A picture is worth a thousand words' is exactly what you are needed to practice by. Such mental images are much easier to recall than written texts as they are vivid in nature. You can also associate symbols and all the senses to the words. For difficult-to-remember words, one can also create acronyms for easier recall. These methods help to encode and decode complex words and messages in an easy fashion.

E. Apply the knowledge you acquire from reading about various subjects. Write down your views and opinions about these subjects. You can either blog your thoughts, contribute to journals, or write reviews of the books you have read, of course by using new words in unique ways.

F. If you are internet-driven, you can visit online dictionaries or even subscribe to word of the day services. Most online dictionaries come with audio features that help you to pronounce new words correctly. They also provide detailed examples to explain the usage of words.

G. Try and link up new words with your existing knowledge and experiences. Analyze the new words by their suffixes and prefixes, or by looking at the pattern of syllables, or by studying their roots. For example, thermometer, thermodynamics and thermostat, all have a common root—thermo, and one can use this root to infer the meaning of newly encountered words which have it as their root.

H. Implicit undertones can also give you a hint about the new word. This habit of analyzing comes in handy when you don't have a thesaurus handy.

I. It is always better to group new words according to their contexts and themes. It is easier to learn and use words and their structure when you associate a meaningful context to them.

J. Create flash cards for new words and use them as much as possible, both in speaking and writing. Slip your new words into conversations; use them in all types of communication settings. This improves the retention rate.

K. Pick up new words through a variety of mediums as this will help you capture terms related to various fields. You could read news online or join an English speaking forum or take active part in role plays.

L. Apart from standard vocabulary lists, build your own vocabulary list. Build it around specific situations, subjects, your profession, or any other dimension that adds practical value to your life. This specific focus helps you to learn faster as you have a clear goal in mind.

M. Hearing a fluent speaker speak is another great method, especially for non-native speakers or learners of English as a second/foreign language.

N. If you are tech-savvy, write a blog or contribute articles. This activity serves two purposes—firstly you improve your vocabulary and secondly you are also able to improve your grammar level.

O. Pick up a standard word list for memorizing words or better still invest in popular books that give you effective techniques for learning new words.

P. Play with new vocabulary. Interactive word games and puzzles like scrabble or crossword puzzles combine pleasure and learning, thus acting as a great motivating factor to enhance knowledge of new words.

Q. Hear it from the horse's mouth. If you have friends who are native speakers of English, it is a great bonus for you. Spend about an hour talking with them. This is a great way of learning new words. This will also let you learn the nuances of the dialect and accent of the spoken word.

R. You could also form a word-learning forum consisting of three to five friends or colleagues. You can use games like Dumb Charades to act out newly learned words.

S. Analogy is an effective way of adding new words to your words vault. Use something familiar to describe something unfamiliar. For example, a skyscraper could be associated with the tall trees in a jungle.

T. A simple exercise is to capture two to three new words daily in your diary along with their definitions, and then learning and using them for the next two to three days in your conversations. Once this is done, at the end of every week, you can ask your friend, colleague or family member to give you the definitions (randomly) and then you can map the correct word against the definitions. This exercise helps you to monitor your word learning process and work on strategies to fill the gaps too.

U. Block out new words from a paragraph that you have learned a few days ago. Read the paragraph carefully and try filling in the blanks by asking comprehension questions. This habit helps not only to recall new words, but also facilitates the development of comprehension skills.

V. Vocabulary exercises in the virtual world are a fun way of enhancing your vocabulary. There are several sites which offer free vocabulary-related quizzes along with useful learning tips.

The techniques are all mental exercises that help to boost your memory power. There are hundreds of techniques for developing a rich vocabulary and thousands of word to learn, but what is important is constant and extensive practice. Select the *right* mix of techniques suited to your learning goals and habits. Mechanical methods like rote learning do not work in the long run. All of us have hundreds of thoughts and ideas streaming through our mental systems, and in what better way can we express them than with a well-stocked vocabulary.

8.6 Basics of Business Correspondence—'Project a Positive Image'

Business correspondence refers to a 2-way communication flow of business information between business stakeholders—internal customers, external customers, suppliers, users and top management. In current times, business transactions have gone global. Production takes place in one/few place/s, but consumption occurs everywhere, and all the information related to this cycle is an *integral* part of communication. Therefore, business correspondence has to be flawless as it helps in the expansion of the business.

Today we live in an age of the Internet, thus there are dynamic changes in the modes of business correspondence. The types of correspondence that we use in the business space are memos, reports, faxes, business letters and E-mails. Whether it is the plain old letter style or hi-tech tools of communication, they both share common rules of thumb. The rules (CROSS) of business correspondence are as follows:

A. Clarity and completeness
B. Relevance and proper references
C. Opening greetings and closing courtesy
D. Simplicity and accuracy
E. Spruce in appearance

As the famous proverb goes "Time is money", business correspondence is one such way of eulogizing this proverb. There are certain basic communication etiquettes to follow in corporate correspondence:

A. **Addressing:** In the case of internal communication, you need to be familiar of the hierarchy level and associated protocols, and use the appropriate level of courtesy. In the case of external correspondence, especially new business contacts, you need to use the highest level of courtesy.

B. **Branding/Company Image:** No matter which medium of communication you use, you need to use it as a means of building your brand and generating goodwill.

C. **Contact names:** Be sure to write the addressee and addressor names formally, full names are a must. Avoid using only first names as this gives the impression that you are hiding something. In E-mail correspondence, be very careful of who goes in the To, Cc and BCc fields. Verify the spelling of all names, first and last.

D. **Direct and point-to-point:** Use direct and active sentences. Keep it simple and do not use jargons. It is best to keep humorous remarks out of the correspondence. Your name and company name should be clearly readable. Your address and other contact details should also be easy to find. Include positive and cordial sentences.

E. **Editing and proofreading:** When sending correspondence, remember to proofread your matter, both electronically and manually. Edit the matter for grammar, style, spelling, tone and content. All these factors depend on the answer to the question 'to whom the correspondence is addressed?' While replying to someone's business correspondence, make sure that you edit and re-edit your response rather than replying in a jiffy. This will ensure that the sender understands and appreciates flawless communication from your end. While replying to business E-mails, ensure that you remove the unwanted E-mail trail, signatures, headers and attachments, and retain matter which is pertinent to your latest response.

F. **Formatting of contents:** You need to take care of date lines, reference lines, addresses, spacing, signatures, margins, enclosures, postscripts, font type and size. Using bold and colored writing is unprofessional. In the case of email programs, the recipient's email software may tend to reject anything out of the normal for spam protection, including bold, colored font types. Apart from these aspects, paper color and paper format is also crucial. Business stationary and company letterhead need to be designed with utmost care as they speak volumes of your company's image and slogan.

G. **Handling conflicts:** This is a major area that is initially handled through business correspondence. Make sure that you deal with facts and figures precisely. Do not let emotions enter the scene. Be firm yet polite in tone. Conflict management is about skilful negotiation. If you are the initiator of the conflict then state your case in clear terms and provide all supporting material. Also specify the timeline within which you expect a resolution. Address the correspondence to appropriate person/department in order to avoid delay. If you are the recipient of the conflict details then be sure that you provide all the facts and escalate the issue to the relevant superiors.

H. **Maintain confidentiality:** If the correspondence is highly sensitive in nature, you need to take appropriate precautions. You must mark the envelope as 'Private and Confidential'. Follow all the guidelines agreed upon in confidentiality agreements between you and recipients.

I. **Placement:** In the case of paper communication, care must be taken of how you place the letter inside the envelope.

J. **References:** Use reference numbers to establish a clear-cut purpose and follow-up guidelines. This helps the recipient to establish a relevant communication context and avoids any sort of misunderstanding.

K. **Signature:** Always end your correspondence with a complete signature. Limit your signature to your name, designation, phone, company name and website. In the case of paper correspondence, do not forget to put a physical signature above your name. This signature adds authenticity to your communication.

L. **Timing factor:** Delay is unacceptable in business communication because all major decisions are time-driven. If there is no explicit reply 'time' window stated, you should always reply as soon as possible. Respond promptly or within the stipulated guidelines.

M. When sending a business communication to people on the same professional level, list their names in alphabetical order. When sending a business communication to people on various professional levels, list them by rank.

The way you correspond and the communication etiquettes you follow have a significant influence on your business image. These factors have become more significant in today's era of international business communication, where you need to deal with business personnel across the globe, on a day-to-day basis.

9 Words in Actions—'Realize the Value of English, Upfront'

Helen Keller, a role model for millions of people, once said that not being able to communicate is more difficult than not being able to see. Words are the immediate gift of God to man. One should be able to verbalize his understanding of the world around him. It needs immense talent to create magic with words, and this magic can be created by realizing the value of the English language, *upfront*. Grind the competition before it grinds you...become an *early adopter* of English. Learning to imitate is a must when it comes to learning a language. That is how we all have learned our native tongues. This quality is distinctly present in children, their young minds are receptive to all sorts of inputs, and hence they are able to learn new skills easily.

Do you usually remain inactive while somebody else carries the conversation? Do you have trouble getting your point across? The most probable reason is that you have learned the language from an exam-focused perspective. No wonder, even after having higher qualifications, many people have difficulty in speaking and writing effectively. When you communicate, you are projecting your SELF. To avoid 'putting your foot in the mouth' situations, you need to gear up for creating your own error-free world with this language. Look at English as an international language of communication, and not as an academic subject. You may have mastered the language from the technical end, but what will make you an upfront beneficiary, is your realization of the importance of the functional aspects associated with this language.

Just as there are several linguistic tools to fine-tune and enrich your language—anecdotes, idioms, metaphors, etc., similarly, there are several reasons why a person would want to learn English, each reason is individual and will provide countless benefits in future. One benefit leads to the other, for example, knowledge of one language facilitates the learning of additional languages.

Knowing the way English works motivates people, especially non-native speakers, to observe their own language and its mechanics in a much better way. The earlier you realize the value of this language, the earlier you will be able to explore the wealth of perceptions and options that it has to offer.

Early learning definitely makes you a culture learner and a successful performer. Apart from this, it lets you develop:

- Functional proficiency
- Cognitive skills
- Improved understanding of native language
- Flexibility and open-mindedness
- Better ear for listening
- Affective skills such as empathy
- Greater appreciation for diversity

9.1 Early Adopters—'It is Not Only About Visuals'

Early adopters are those people who realize the value of English, *upfront*. The formula to success is simple: if one realizes the importance and benefits of something, one will try harder to learn it and that too with continued interest. The same holds true for English. Open-mindedness should also be exercised to sustain the interest level.

A man is known by the words he speaks. English is loaded with phrases, metaphors, alliterations, similes, anecdotes and idioms. These not only enhance your communicative effectiveness with resonant imagery, but also act as great verbal devices. With these devices, the recipient/s of your message will see, understand, interpret, respond, and remember you and your message, in a much better way.

Mere exposure to this language is not enough. Repeated use of English is what will make you a successful language learner, and eventually a critical thinker and successful performer in this diverse society. In this knowledge-based era, you will need to master power-packed words and expressions so that you make people see and feel exactly what you want them to.

> **Spotlight**
> Early adopters gain competitive advantage from learning English. They also realize that they have roots like all others do, and not only develop respect for their own roots, but also treat people and their roots with compassion and empathy.

9.1.1 An example of effective communication—'Effective is the key'

People and organizations with effective English communication skills perform three times better than their counterparts with poor communication abilities.

Effective communication in English simply means the following **Five Ss**, which are applicable in all spheres of life—personal, social and professional.

(a) **Structure:** The structure of the communication content will largely be determined by the target audience and the environment.

(b) **Study:** Study and analyze the purpose of the message to be communicated. This will help you structure your message appropriately and deliver it in concise and crisp terms. In order to determine the exact way of delivering the message, the urgency factor also needs to be examined.

(c) **Settings:** The environment needs to be taken into consideration too. Adapt your communication style, delivery timing and language to the settings. Know your domain well in order to use the right forms of the language. For example, in an informal setting, you can use jargons and idiomatic expressions.

(d) **Supporting elements:** Supporting elements like body language, verbal devices, tone and facial expressions play an important role too. Your voice is a great tool, so employ it to deliver your very best. Communication is not merely about messages; it is also about brand building and appropriate behaviors.

(e) **Straight feedback:** Seek feedback inputs and follow-up on the message communicated to ensure whether the recipient has understood your message or not.

Another thumb rule is to avoid the following factors—unnecessary words, clichés, slang, assumptions, information overload and prejudices.

The bottom line, however, is in knowing the grammar; in knowing how to use the various forms of the language. This knowing is the difference between communicating and communicating *perfectly*.

Here is an example of a constructive business conversation—call center complaint registration system.

Representative: Good Morning. How can I help you Sir?

Customer: Hello. I am facing trouble with my landline instrument.

Representative: I am extremely sorry for the inconvenience caused. May I have your customer number please?

Customer: Sure, my customer number is VV85475405845.

Representative: Kindly describe the exact problem?

Customer: The display unit is not functioning. It shows up a blank screen.

Representative: Give me a moment please. I am generating your complaint/request number. Don't worry Sir. I have registered your problem details.

Customer: By when is it likely to be solved?

Representative: Please take down your complaint number. Sir, I assure you that the problem will be resolved by our technician within the next 24 hours. Is there anything else that you need help with?

Customer: No. Thank you very much for your assistance.

Representative: Thank you for calling. Have a nice day.

Customer: Goodbye.

9.1.2 Key Points—'Prepare, rehearse, anticipate and respond'

Key points: Company personnel/representatives are required to address customer problems with patience and empathy. Customers, in turn, need to talk with politeness and explain their concerns in non-nebulous words.

Preparation before communication: Prepare and rehearse mentally what you want to convey. Anticipate responses and questions from the other party, and then reply accordingly. Based on the knowledge and background of the recipient/s, encode the message you want to convey in relevant terms.

Beginning of the communication cycle: All the stakeholders involved in the communication cycle need to begin the cycle on a pleasant note by exchanging greetings and following protocols.

During the communication: Each one involved in the give and take of communicative content needs to ensure that a healthy, positive environment is maintained. A bias-free environment is necessary for decoding messages correctly. Empathy is another important aspect that ensures messages are not misinterpreted, and are correctly understood.

End of the communication cycle: All the communicators need to end the communication cycle on an affirmative note. Everyone needs to ensure that valuable information and feedback are shared, and in turn are used to bring about a positive outcome.

The knowledge of English helps to lock together all the phases of the communication cycle. It helps you to learn from and act upon the feedback/information received.

9.2 The Anecdotal Story—'Guess the Name Game'

Anecdotes or modern-day parables are superb verbal devices, which help you to bring character and add depth to the communication content. They are perfect replacements for bland statements. They play a major role in making speeches and presentations a success. Their main aim is to convey the subject, reason or lesson through short stories or personal experiences. Let me offer you some food for thought.

Anecdote: The Braille system was developed by Louis Braille, a blind Frenchman. Beethoven composed his greatest works after becoming deaf. John Bunyan wrote Pilgrim's Progress in jail. Helen Keller was the first deaf and blind person to earn a bachelor's degree in Arts.

Can you infer the inspirational message that I am conveying through the anecdote?

I am sure people fluent in English have their answer ready and full marks to them. People who are not that English-friendly, may not be able to relate to the essence of the underlying pearl of wisdom. I am sure these people are aware of the power of persistent efforts to overcome all the adversities in life, but due to the language barriers, are not able to understand the emotive power of this anecdote.

Whether you are writing a non-fiction book or appearing for a job interview, anecdotes help you to pull things together. They are present in each and every aspect of our lives. You can find them in something that someone told you, in newspapers or in your workplace too. They not only make your communication thought-provoking, interesting and engaging, but also add the personal dimension to it.

The bottom line

Without the basic knowledge of this language, it is hard to survive in current times, where overall growth and success can be enjoyed only by connecting with the whole world. The use of anecdotes facilitates the practice of language skills and they also energize your skills (listening, writing, comprehending, speaking and thinking) thereby making your communication content easier to comprehend and more accessible to the others. At the same time, the recipient of anecdotes also needs the English backing in order to infer the valuable message/values embedded in the anecdote and relate them to their own life.

9.3 The Idiom Story—'Understand the Implied Meaning'

Idioms symbolize a set of age-old values and moral teachings. They have cultural significance embedded in them, which helps to pass on ancient wisdom from one generation to the other.

They are one of the most enjoyable ways to produce meaningful content.

Idioms in your English usage is not about making the language sound flowery, but rather it goes to show that you know how to use the idioms to emphasize the meaning of the context or situation, *effectively*. An extensive vocabulary backed with the knowledge of idioms would help one and all to achieve 'outstanding' success.

9.3.1 Lesson 7—'It is good to be idiomatic'

The idiom 'A little bird told me' means a secret or a private source of information.

Illustration 9.1: Idioms can Help You to Get Out of a Tight Spot

In the illustration, the man on the right does not really want to reveal the details and at the same time, he does not want to sound rude. In order to avoid any clash or misunderstanding, he uses an idiom to give his answer. Now it is an altogether different story that the man on the left does not really know the implied meaning of the idiom (idioms can both get you out of and put you in a tight spot), and that is why there is a bird of confusion fluttering over his head.

Judicious usage of idioms in your writing assignments or speaking engagements, adds flavor and an interesting tone. Idioms in your language arsenal indicate a higher level of fluency in the English language.

A non-native speaker may not understand the context of the idiom or may misinterpret the idiom expression. At times, idioms can turn out to be a source of 'cultural shock' for non-native speakers. Let me share with you some tips to build up your base of idioms: an idiom a day keeps errors away, exposure to communication with native speakers, enjoy the process of learning, and associate a story/keyword with idioms.

9.3.2 Fill in the blanks—'Fun with colors'

A. Penny has a wonderful garden. She surely has __ fingers.

B. The burglar was caught __ handed.

C. The grass is always __ on the other side of the fence.

D. We experience a torrential downpour once in a __ moon.

E. Never give up. Look at life and its lessons through __ glasses.

F. He is always treated like a __ sheep.

9.4 Facts—'Strange But True'

A. The most commonly used word in written English is *the*.

B. Words like cattle, trousers and clothes are all plural but have no singular form.

C. The following are some conflicting proverbs. My word of advice is that take everything with a pinch of salt. After all, these are age-old words of wisdom.

Opposites attract	↔ Birds of a feather flock together
What will be, will be	↔ Life is what you make it
Ignorance is bliss	↔ Knowledge is power

D. Negatives without positives are words with no positive forms. For example, inert and invert.

E. What is so strange but true about the following sentence?

"The quick brown fox jumps over the lazy dog".

Do you want me to spill the beans? Well, it is just a matter of accurate observation and nothing more than that. This sentence is a pangram. A pangram is a sentence that contains all the alphabets of English language.

9.5 Questions for Reflection

1. If you are planning to implement an early language learning program in your city, what challenges would you need to consider?
2. Do you think that some individuals are naturally talented when it comes to second language acquisition?
3. Do you think verbal tools integrated into the classroom sessions can prove useful to establish a meaningful environment for learning the English language?

9.6 Chapter Recap

A. It needs immense talent to create magic with words, and this magic can be created by realizing the value of the English language, *upfront*.

B. Look at English as an international language of communication, and not as an academic subject. You may have mastered the language from the technical end, but what will make you an upfront beneficiary, is your realization of the importance of the functional aspects of it.

C. Use verbal devices like metaphors, similes and anecdotes to connect with your audience, to reinforce a critical point or to bring energy to the process of communication.

D. Without the basic knowledge of this language, it is hard to survive in current times.

E. Mere exposure to this language is not enough. Repeated use of English is what will make you a successful language learner, and eventually a critical thinker and successful performer in this diverse society.

F. Effective communication in English simply means the following **Five Ss**—structure, study, settings, supporting elements and straight feedback, which are applicable in all spheres of life—personal, social and professional.

G. Idioms in your English usage is not about making the language sound flowery, but rather it goes to show that you know how to use the idioms to emphasize the meaning of the context or situation, *effectively*. An extensive vocabulary backed with the knowledge of idioms would help one and all to achieve 'outstanding' success.

English Today and Tomorrow—'Future Perfect English' 10

Broaden your mental horizon
And adopt an international outlook
By getting into 'English' action.

All languages are constantly evolving to meet new communicative needs, and English is no exception to this rule. English is constantly evolving and will continue to evolve and adapt itself to the needs of its users. It will continue to change to keep abreast of latest technologies, world events and people experiences. Today's English is different from the English of 100 years ago, and no doubt, it will be even more different in 100 years' time. As I stated earlier, English as a language is evolving all the time, and it is wise to evolve along with it.

Any local language gives a sense of identity, whereas English provides the means to global growth and the dimension of interculturality. The moment the local aspect starts to become powerful, the situation of English could become dicey. While speaking of the future trends of English, all we can do is instead of predicting in a baseless way, we should speculate with caution.

To be a part of this process of evolvement, one needs to play an active role in the ever-changing configuration of the speakers of the English language in the world.

Giving up the opportunity to learn English due to language biases, cultural identity crisis or irrational sentimental urges, is utter foolishness. Look at it this way, no matter what the global future will be, by learning English at least you are trying to secure your future.

> **Spotlight**
> English will change and evolve without fail, and those who do not change and evolve with it, will be left behind.

USA exercises a greater influence on the way English is developing worldwide than any other nation. Hence, the future of this nation is bound to play a major role in determining the future role and status of English.

The never-ending debate between making English as the official language and not making it will continue into the future too. There are several factors in this space, which need to be kept track of in order to predict the future of English. Factors like education programs, complexity and cost of introducing laws, immigration rate, people's motivation level to adopt English and many more socio-eco-political factors will determine who wins, whether the anti-official supporters or the pro-official supporters.

10.1 Future in India—'From *Angrezi* to English'

Whether it is the diplomats
Or the youth generation,
Everyone uses English in this nation.

India became an independent nation in 1947, and the English language was supposed to be phased out by 1965. But that did not happen at all. We all know that today English and Hindi have equal importance in Indian affairs. English in India has, indeed, come a long way from its original status in the British Raj times when it was mostly used as the language of the administration.

English has influenced India since the early 1600's, when the East India Company started trading. Remember, the dialog for independence too was conducted in English. The demand for English language training, education and services is on an ever-increasing rise. Post-independence, the focus of the curriculum of English studies has slowly and steadily shifted from teaching British specific literature to using English as a medium of instruction. Now, this language is studied by "decolonized minds".

Today, English in India has practically become the backbone of the higher education system. It is not looked at as 'colonial baggage' anymore. Several major institutions like the Regional

English Language Office (RELO), based in Delhi, have been set up to promote the effective teaching of English. Another milestone event that reflects the importance of English in India is the Commonwealth Games 2010. This major event had triggered a chain reaction of linguistic image makeovers amongst Delhi drivers/conductors. They went through an extensive revamp in terms of honing their English speaking skills. Subsequently, they dealt with foreign players and tourists, both effectively and politely.

Now, even after more than 60 years of independence, English remains the associate official language along with Hindi, which is the official language. More momentum was added by the liberalization of the Indian economy in the 1990s.

Although currently Indian English is highly influenced by its American counterpart, it is surely taking big leaps in its own way. In times to come, as India gains economic momentum, Indian English will also make its impact felt beyond the Indian borders.

Table 10.1: English Speakers by Country

Rank	Country	Number
#1	United States	280,000,000
#2	India	100,000,000
#3	United Kingdom	55,000,000

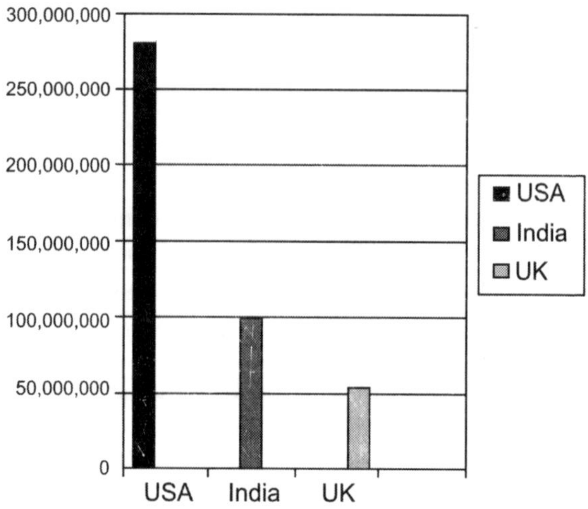

Figure 10.1: English Speakers by Country

The bar diagram (Figure 10.1) clearly shows that Indians are very much aware of the advantages of being fluent in English.

Spectacular breakthroughs, hi-tech technological advancements, and access to several language learning tools and methods like online learning software programs are adding to the number of literates in the Indian subcontinent.

The Indian workforce is omnipresent; you will find an Indian in every nook and corner of the world. Indians know the importance of English when it comes to operating in the global space, and at the same time, they are also instrumental in popularizing Indianized English words, which we all refer to as Hinglish. The sheer numbers of Hinglishmen in the corporate world in general and in the Information Technology space in particular, makes it inevitable that some Hinglish words will get globalized.

India ranks third in the publication of English books, immediately after the United States and United Kingdom. This goes to show that the publishing industry for English books is surely *linguistically* exciting.

India's proposal to establish regional English Language Centers was well received by the 11th ASEAN Summit held in 2005.

Just as the case with the world scenario, communication technology, literacy levels, opportunities for growth will certainly affect the linguistic trends in India as well.

It is interesting to note that India is not only being influenced by the English wave, but also it plays a major role in the growth of the language. Two major facts that make India play this vital role are as follows:

- India is second in terms of number of English-speaking persons. There are more people speaking English in India than in the rest of the native English-speaking nations of the world.
- India is a major player in the Information Technology and Business Process Outsourcing space. One global example would be that of call centers. If you connect

to a call center anywhere in the world, including India, often you will get to hear an Indian voice at the other end of the phone. People in India tend to have very good English skills, which gives them an advantage for outsourcing when compared to other Asian countries, where the workforce may not be as well-versed in English as their Indian counterparts.

> **Spotlight**
>
> To expand the global point of view, to establish peaceful ties with nations, and to capitalize on social, economic and political opportunities, India needs to allocate appropriate funds and resources for English language planning.

Major institutions like the British Council have introduced massive projects in India for providing best resources from the UK for English teaching, and one such example is Project English. It was introduced in India in 2007, with an aim to provide quality teaching and training, right from primary learners to corporate users of this language.

In spite of the sharp dip in the number of test-takers due to the economic slowdown, India remains one of the most prominent countries taking up language tests like TOEFL.

10.2 The Linguistic Future of the Wired World—'English-Savvy Net Users'

Gear up for technology-based
Language acquisition
In order to establish your position.

In the initial days of the wired world, more than 90 per cent of the early users of the Internet were located in the United States. Today, the trend of making one's presence felt in the virtual space is growing fastest in developing countries—China and India. Even countries like Italy and Brazil have a high English-savvy net population.

Hi-tech advancements are resulting in more people from around the world learning English. The very nature of the wired world is changing on a daily basis, and we are only at the beginning of this revolution. English is a vehicle of knowledge transmission, but now, with knowledge being Internet-driven, English plays yet another critical role—expansion of the knowledge base. This dual role of transmission and expansion leads to broader technological, religious, cultural, political and economic exchanges. This in turn increases the number of producers and consumers of knowledge, *exponentially*.

The hybrid versions of English are and will continue affecting English online. Though today English is the *lingua franca* of the Internet, what will determine its status from a few years from now, is the rate of local language momentum, translation services and localization support.

These hybrid versions of English are steadily increasing their presence on the Internet. For example, one of the most searched topics on the Internet in China is MBA courses, where the search string 'mba课程' is used to perform the search operation. Similarly, in other nations, such local English words are picking up. Now, the rate of this spread will be determined by how companies working in this domain capitalize on this trend.

English web content may continue to dominate the virtual space even as English first-language Internet users decline. At the same time, we cannot overrule the possibility that the use of English websites could decline as alternatives in other languages become available.

The wired world is becoming more multilingual, but a truly multilingual WWW is a far-fetched dream, and will certainly take time and efforts to realize the same. In the meanwhile, English will continue to remain the main language of the online world. It is interesting to note that WWW = World Wide Web = Three English Words.

10.3 Global Trends—'Where does English Go from Here'

> English is the first tongue
> To go global in the true sense.
> It connects one and all by the click of a mouse.

Experts predict by 2015 half the world's population will be speaking or at least learning English. By 2030 and beyond, it is predicted that the number of people who speak English as a second or foreign language will exceed the number of native speakers, much more than now. This trend will continue to grow. The widespread use of English will continue to bring about global uniformity.

As has been stated earlier, USA being a major political and economic player will largely determine the future roadmap of English. Shift in political and economic power results in new language loyalties, and this is possible only when major nations like USA lose their stronghold to others. If the entire English-speaking population of a particular small nation decides to switch from English to their native language, this would have a negligible impact on English.

As English is the vehicle for communication, more local varieties could develop as and when it comes in contact with new regions. This means, the usage of English which is suited to the local taste, and the use of local languages for international communication.

In the world of business, focus has constantly been on shifting from the realization of a product/service-based vision to deriving value through language communication on a worldwide basis. In current times, you will notice that the focus is more on deriving value and providing a satisfying customer experience, and all this is possible by conveying the right kind of USP, and of course through the right medium—English. The proportion of value derived from products and services through language-related communication is on the rise.

English gives flesh to local ideas, and this gives them an international appeal. Each and every language is a vehicle of expression and a wealth of wisdom. If we look at English in a positive way and not as a threat to other languages, we will realize how English can be used as an effective means of promoting local/regional views of life on a global level and for strengthening our cultural ties with the rest of the world.

10.3.1 Lesson 8—'Go global'

The illustration depicts another major trend, even students of English are aware that English is not merely English in the

Queens's land but it is about English in the 'global village', which is spoken everywhere by everyone. Gone are the days, when it was feasible for you to 'think local and act global', now it is all about 'think global and act global'.

Illustration 10.1: Speaking Globish is a Big Trend

10.3.2 Views on the Future of English Survey—'Majority said Yes'

I interviewed 250 people from various walks of life, over a period of three months, about their views on the future of English. And the one major question I posed to them was 'Will English retain its global status and will it continue to grow in popularity?'

234 said yes, 12 answered in negation and only 4 respondents said they were not sure. The following figure is the bar diagram

representing the composite responses of the interviewees divided into three main categories: Yes, No and Not sure.

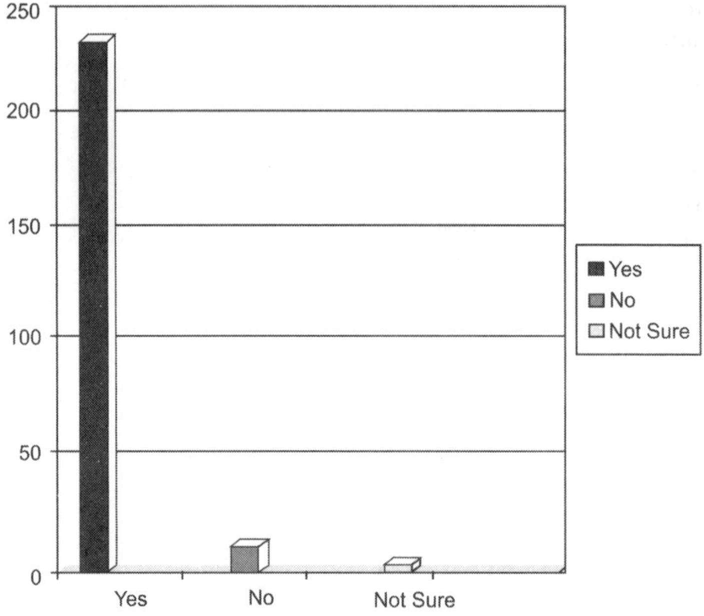

Figure 10.2: Results of the Future of English Survey

10.3.3 Trends and Challenges—'No fun without them'

Another growing trend is that large segments of the world workforce are taking to advanced higher-level English education. This in turn will result in the increase of mobility of the knowledge economy.

The turn of the 19th century has made English a 'Star' language. Rich history and traditions in the form of folktales, idioms, folk music and many other aspects provide a unique view of our world. Indeed, English is not just a language but a repository of history, literature, science, arts and cultural identity as well.

Political upheavals or economic revolutions may have a marginal effect on the status of English as it is not owned by any single country anymore. What could be a possible threat to this dominance are artificial intelligence setups, where people communicate in their first languages and computers translate it into the desired languages. But again, this is going to take time. Real-time translation is still in the initial phases and it will take it quite a while to match up with its human counterparts. Even support for linguistic features like idioms and expressions is minimal in machine translations. Though breakthroughs in this space are occurring at a steady rate, it is going to take a long period to have a global impact. Thus, it is too early to predict what influence artificial systems will have on the position of English.

There are several factors that will need to be studied from time to time in order to determine what course the English language is going to take. One major aspect is the views and attitudes that people hold towards this language.

The American hold over science and technology will need to be closely watched in order to determine the status of English from time to time.

Another important determining factor is economics and demographics. In the 21st century, the spread of and linguistic allegiance towards English will be decided by economics and demographics. Political factors will also influence the direction that English takes, in their own unique way. Economics and demographics, the level of migration, the degree of urbanization, and the spread of English-oriented education will determine the following aspects:

- Whether English will replace other languages?
- Whether English will be replaced by other languages?
- Whether English will be able to sustain competition from local varieties?

In the future, it is quite likely that English will be salted with more local dialects and also result in pidgins influenced by non-native speakers. These new flavors may eventually have to be learned by native English speakers if they want to participate in global affairs.

All these factors together will determine whether more and more dialects will fuse into English to form one common flavor, or English will have local versions due to economic and political shifts in power.

With countries like China, which are also consciously making efforts to spread their own language across the world, we are already witnessing multi-linguistic trends with English still playing a major role rather than its current bi-linguistic position. In order to meet the demands of these new trends, native English speakers will need to step out of their comfort zone. They will need to be attuned to the multi-linguistic trends in order to operate efficiently in the global arena.

Things can change, and they actually do, often with unpredictable speed and in the opposite direction. Yes, English has become a necessity today, but no one knows what will happen tomorrow. 'Being prepared' is the magic *mantra*.

There is no doubt that English is used on a global scale, but for it to be a permanent universal reality, it will need to overcome many linguistic challenges. Some of the challenges that English may have to face:

A. The position of English will depend on how well it is managed across the world in terms of its status and learning policy.

B. How will English protect its status against attacks from nations trying real hard to protect their identity by not giving in to English?

C. The level of willingness shown by English-speaking people to be attuned to the multi-linguistic trends. Will they step out of their comfort zone?

D. The growth and progress of nations like Japan, India, China, which have the largest population numbers.

E. Alternative economic scenarios where countries may not want to participate in the global economy, instead focus their resources on their local economies.

F. The immigration explosion versus identity preservation.

G. Major changes in the economic profile, balance of power and military assertiveness.

We also cannot rule out the possibility of linguistic imperialism. Given the scale of the global reach that this language enjoys, it may result in 'language deaths' or 'linguicides' of several minority languages. This could also widen the rift between the rich and the poor as the rich have the resources to gain knowledge of this language.

According to several linguists and language planners, the immersion of English is so deep that the language won't die out and it is unlikely to be unseated from its perch atop the linguistic landscape anytime soon, but what will happen is that Standard English will coexist with its diversified dialects. An implication from this viewpoint is that a native English speaker might need to become bilingual in his own language to converse with other speakers of global English. I find this viewpoint extremely exciting.

A Word of Caution

No matter what the future of the English language is, but for those of you who wish to influence the future, must prepare for it.

Since there has never been a language with such a global reach and magnitude, one does not know what really happens to such a language in the future. As there are no historical precedents, one cannot predict the future of English with absolute accuracy. One can only make guesstimates. Again, close and on-going study and observation of geopolitical changes and demographic transitions will be needed to track the future of this language.

We cannot forget the most important factor that influences the status of English—the speakers of this language. The speakers who govern the use and spread of English will need to be closely studied. Any change in their attitudes is going to affect English, either favorably or unfavorably. Thus, speakers of English and the factors discussed will determine the future course of this language.

In my opinion, any language will be truly global when it is not owned by any particular nation or governed by any particular international body, or when it is not influenced by geopolitical forces. Any challenger of the English language will first need to reverse the impact of English, only then it can try to gain global prominence. The challenging language will also need to have promising factors (cultural, social, economic, psychological and linguistic) to be able to motivate people to acquire the new language.

10.4 What Next?—'My Two Cents'

The answer is simple: Learning more than one language is always better.

Predicting the future course of the English language is synonymous to the famous quote 'To be or not to be'. In either case, I suggest the following course for you all....

After you have mastered the English language, it is time to put your knowledge to test. Take a break and vacation in UK or US. Go ahcad and enjoy yourself! You will then realize how many opportunities you have been missing out on, all this while.

With English in your vacation luggage, your vacation experience will prove to be a fulfilling and enriching one.

I also have a few topics for Ph.D. students, which can be used for their dissertation projects, and in turn give us more insights into the dynamics of this language—analysis of the competition of American English (AmE) and British English (BrE), or modern methods of English acquisition, or you could even pick any one of the questions in the 'Questions for Reflection' subtopic, from any of the chapters in this book.

ALL THE BEST.

HAPPY LEARNING!

10.5 Questions for Reflection

1. Will English retain its position in the 21st century?
2. What role will English play in language shifts caused due to globalization?
3. Will it be popular even in 2050 when countries like China and India are likely to be super powers?
4. What role can English play in shaping the future of Indian youth?

5. What impact will the revolution of the wired world have on the evolution of English?

10.6 Chapter Recap

A. Any local language gives a sense of identity, whereas English provides the means to global growth and the dimension of interculturality.

B. While speaking of the future trends of English, all we can do is instead of predicting in a baseless way, we should speculate with caution.

C. Although currently Indian English is highly influenced by its American counterpart, it is surely taking big leaps in its own way. In times to come, as India gains economic momentum, Indian English will also make its impact felt beyond the Indian borders.

D. Though today English is the *lingua franca* of the Internet, what will determine its status from a few years from now, is the rate of local language momentum, translation services and localization support.

E. English is a vehicle of knowledge transmission, but now, with knowledge being Internet-driven, English plays yet another critical role—expansion of the knowledge base. This dual role of transmission and expansion leads to broader technological, religious, cultural, political and economic exchanges.

F. The turn of the 19th century has made English a 'Star' language. Rich history and traditions in the form of folktales, idioms, folk music and many other aspects provide a unique view of our world. Indeed, English is not just a language but a repository of history, literature, science, arts and cultural identity.

G. There are several factors like attitudes of people, political upheavals and economic revolutions that will need to be studied from time to time in order to determine what course the English language is going to take.

H. The most important factor that influences the status of English—the speakers of this language. The speakers who govern the use and spread of English will need to be closely studied. Any change in their attitudes is going to affect English, either favorably or unfavorably.

Bonus Bytes—'Get the Edge' 11

Here is a chapter from my book on personal transformation—*The 6 Spheres of Life: Unlocking the Door to Success and Happiness*. This mini chapter gives you a proven formula and easily doable tips to get that competitive edge by achieving proficiency in English.

11.1 The EDGE Formula for Honing the English Language Skills

As we all know that we are living in the world of globalization, and effective communication using the universal language—English is the key for survival in this age of globalization. No wonder, English is known as the *lingua franca* of the modern civilization. It is that language which has unified people from all walks of life and cultures into a seamless global village.

Poor communication can affect all aspects of life. It can lead to business loss, misunderstandings and inferiority complex. The usage of English permeates every single aspect of life, be it addressing a board room meeting or appearing for an interview or even while placing a telephonic product order. Though English is not an official language in many countries, yet at the global level, it is the most widely used language for all sorts of correspondence—written, spoken, or electronic. English being the common mode of communication, it is of utmost importance to be well-versed in it. English is very important for personality development, which is yet another important aspect for raising the success ratio. The EDGE formula will help you develop your English speaking, thinking, writing, reading and listening skills.

Essential knowledge of grammar.
Develop all aspects of the language.
Gain fluency.
Enhance the language skills by practice and examples.

The base of any language is its grammar and that base is something that we all need to master, to learn the language fluently. Even a small grammatical error can cause a bad impression and convey an incorrect meaning. English grammar is much simpler and easier to pick up as compared to many other languages. Ensure that you approach the grammar open mindedly, do not relate the grammar rules of your native language with that of English. There are certain rules and regulations for each and every topic in grammar of this language, if adopted correctly, flawless communication is bound to follow. Apart from the usual route of joining a language learning program, one can always include the following useful tips for improving English grammar:

1. Review your grammar from time to time. Rather than trying to be perfect all the time, instead concentrate on one set of mistakes first; improve them and then move on to the next.
2. Analyzing the context of the situation will help you frame grammatically correct sentences. It will also help you use the right tense to apply to the verbs in the sentences.
3. Online grammar puzzles, grammar exercise books can also help.
4. Identify common mistakes that people make, as most of the times, it is quite likely that you too are committing the same mistakes. Refer to grammar text books or seek advice from a language tutor to correct these mistakes. For example, most people in the initial learning stage are confused as to which article to use—a, an, or the.
5. Visual aids like charts and tables can help to reinforce the rules.

As I mentioned earlier, gaining mastery of English (for that matter any other language too) includes writing, listening, talking, thinking and reading. Ensure that all these aspects make heavy use of this language. Let me illustrate with examples:

1. Update your personal timetable or personal diary in English instead of doing so in your mother tongue. Over time you will be able to express yourself fluently. Don't let minor obstructions bog you down.
2. Apart from listening to news in your first language, listen to English news channels or watch the Discovery channel. This exercise serves a dual purpose—it adds to the vocabulary and also improves your general awareness.
3. Make concerted efforts to communicate with your family, friends or colleagues in English. Initially, you could probably decide to communicate using English for only 5 hours. You can steadily increase this time once you feel more comfortable. You can take extracts from famous speeches and rehearse the same in front of the mirror. At the same time, you could record yourself on the tape, and re-listen to the recording. This will help you identify pronunciation mistakes and improve your listening skills as well.
4. Even when you are self-reflecting or thinking, use English to converse with yourself and frame your thoughts. This habit will help you handle complex real life situations where the English language is the main mode of communication.
5. This is one tip that each one of us is familiar with. Read quality magazines and books so that you can hone your language, improve your vocabulary and avoid learning slang words. Various software programs are also available to aid you in this activity.

As English is the universal language of business communication, fluency in this language is of utmost importance.

In combination with the previous techniques, one can use the following techniques to enhance the fluency level:

1. Find native English-speaking people who will give you conversation practice. If this is not possible then at least find someone who is well-versed in English and who can guide you correctly if you go wrong.
2. Make it a habit to add 2-3 new words to your vocabulary vault. Also learn to use them in conversation so that you don't forget them. You could pick up these words from various sources like newspapers, from a friend or even a billboard.
3. Business communication does not just entail presentations or board room meetings. You could start small by ensuring that your casual conversations are perfect in all aspects—structure, sentences, accent, frame and tone. Once you are comfortable with this fluency level, you can move onto the next. One advantage of casual conversations is that you will get instant feedback from your colleagues and you can work on the same to correct yourself.
4. Focusing on the inflections, rhythm, the unpronounced letters and syllables is also an important aspect of ensuring that you present yourself perfectly. One way to work on these aspects is listening to fluent speakers of English on a regular basis.

The fourth point of this formula is basically an amalgamation of all the above tips and techniques combined with regular practice and feedback. This formula attempts to tell you that gaining proficiency in any language, including English, is about mastering grammar, vocabulary, pronunciation, nuances and fluency. A large part of what you will achieve in your life will depend on your comfort level with this language. This formula will help you achieve that comfort level.

Open the doors to global opportunities
Using the key of English.
Get an EDGE over the others!

Real Life Quotes—'Useful Insights'

12

Here are quotes shared by professionals working in various fields, right from authors to managers, from teachers to motivational speakers, about their experiences with the English language. You will find useful insights as to why these people, both native and non-native speakers of English, strived for excellence in English skills, and how these persistent efforts helped them to scale new heights of growth and success in their respective professions as well as personal lives.

A. "Pushing" the English Language in My Writing to New Dimensions of Thought and Feeling: Symbolism and metaphor have become useful extensions of more academic writing that characterized my writing over the first half of my life and career. I have wanted to "push" the English language to open readers to new dimensions of thought, and more critically, feeling and awareness. I was greatly influenced by Carl Jung's notion of symbolism, using more metaphoric language to convey dynamic realities I have wanted to portray. For example, "Initiating" is a term I use in my team development work to suggest the initial rite of passage of a person or persons unfamiliar with each other, moving through a threshold to become more vulnerable and authentic, achieving greater understanding, then trust, and then belonging (see *Building Team Spirit*, 1997, McGraw Hill). I have done this through the use of symbolic imagery, for example, the use of a spiral graphic to illustrate the interdependent dimensions necessary to developing and manifesting purpose as highly organic, interdependent elements of the Noble Purpose Spiral (see *Noble Purpose, Igniting Extraordinary Passion for Life and Work*, 2004, QSU Publishers).

—Dr. Barry Heermann (USA),
Author, Educator and Organizational Consultant

B. Although I do not have a convent school background, I had an avid interest towards English since my childhood days. Whenever I visit my relatives, I enquire about the latest English books, journals and books on translation, phonetics, etc. When I visit metros like Delhi, Mumbai or Kolkata, I always am in search of quality English books. On Sundays I visit local bookstores to collect books for my personal library, especially books on spirituality, poetry, philosophy, biography, travelogue, psychology like Dale Carnegie books and books on meditation and yoga. I happen to be a voracious reader and a good listener too. I listen to good speakers of history like Kennedy, Nehru, Disraeli, Carter and to many British Premiers, UN Secretary Generals, novelists, poets, and philosophers to enhance and rectify my speaking essence in English.

After becoming the editor of *The Eternity*, since 2005, I am in touch with poets, authors, and writers from across the world. And now I have to write to them, speak with them, and interact with them, regularly. I have to review several books and edit poetry entries for the journal, all of them are in English. Thus, English has been my sincere companion, always. My responsibility has been enhanced as I have to translate many spiritual writings from Hindi for the English readers in any part of the world. My research areas include meditation, yoga and super consciousness, and for me to share my findings with the rest of the world, I need English. I have to write many books with my experiences in English for the readers across the world and for the welfare of humankind. English is a world language and the right medium to preach any good lessons for mankind. The world can be awakened through English, spiritually. We all know Swami Vivekananda, Sri Aurobindo, Rabindranath Tagore, in their times, could influence the world because of their access to English. And, that is the reason why Tagore could be the first Nobel laureate in literature from Asia in 1913.

—Harekrushna Mahanta, IWA,
Publisher, Editor, *The Eternity Literary Journal*

C. The world is rapidly shrinking. Family, friends, clients, and customers are no longer right down the street or even still in our city. But thanks to technology and the ability of so many people to understand the English language, they are still easily accessible.

Being proficient in the English language allows us to communicate with almost anyone, almost anywhere in the world. This truly is remarkable because we can finally meet people who we only read about in our newspapers or heard about on the news. We no longer hear just about the calamities and the crises, but the catastrophes and the horrors as well. We meet everyday people and see firsthand that they are just like us.

I truly believe that technology combined with knowledge of the English language will help bring more understanding and peace to our world. We are not limited to what we hear on the news. When I hear about volcanoes, or tidal waves, or earthquakes, I check the maps to see if any of my friends or customers is in harm's way and pray that they and their families and friends are okay. It's not obscure anymore. It's not something happening "to those people over there". It's something happening in a country or city where I know every day people who are trying to make the best out of their lives just like most every other person in the world.

—Ms. Grace Adele,
Managing Editor, Bristol Banner Books (USA)

D. When I started writing in Hindi (in my teens) I didn't have any competence in English. I was a Hindi medium student and there was no environment to learn good English whether at home or in the college. Soon I discovered that I won't be able to make any impact through my journalistic, poetic or fiction writing in Hindi— there was so much politics and competition, and no mentor to promote me even if I used to appear in almost every daily and weekly published from Varanasi in those days—I dabbled in writing in English. As a student in BA I thought my English was good and I could write poetry in English. I was wrong. My literature teachers, too, discouraged me from wasting my energy in writing in English. But the more they found fault with my writing, the more determined I became to write and publish in English. With continued failures in the seventies, I did succeed, after I became lecturer in English and gradually learnt how to find my rhythm and edit my poetry and/or write what most others won't dare to.

Poetry came to me naturally when thinking in English had become normal and I had to teach English language rather than literature. I learnt to write with no or minimum adjectives; I learnt to be brief and without being wasteful; I learnt to write with a sense of rhythm. It was good that I did not read T.S. Eliot or the Romantics or the Victorians after becoming a teacher, nor did I need to teach any authors I studied in BA or MA. I taught 'English for Science and Technology' and professionally concentrated on 'specific purposes' language teaching rather than teaching even modern or contemporary literature.

Because my forgetting is faster than remembering, so I always had something new to write or think about. I didn't have the support of any of the big names in Indian English writing, so I kept on doing what I have been doing all these years just as promoting the less known/unknown poets became my passion. I am happy today more new authors are being talked about than it was thirty years ago. Even for research (here at ISM) I promote new or less known authors and poets and leave the old or established ones for others to deal with.

With the emergence of the internet and several international print journals becoming electronic journals, I have been regularly posting my poems on various literary sites and it is gratifying that my writing in English is now more accessible globally. I won't die an unknown name and one or the other search engine will mention one or the other of my books or poems in English (as also in other languages).

—Dr. R.K. Singh,
University Professor of English, Author,
Critic, Reviewer and ELT/EST Practitioner

E. English is no doubt becoming a very preferred and popular language in today's world, not only in corporate, but even in personal life. This is surely an impact of globalization. Technology has brought the world very close and mediums like Internet, mobile phones, GPS, etc., have made communication very fast and swift. To keep pace with the growing economy and new technology, English is becoming more of a mandatory language for successful survival in today's times of tough competition.

Personally I realized it during my career progression as well. As I grew in my career, the need to refine English emerged at every stage, since all the positions I have been heading so far always demanded refined communication skills. This never acted as a barrier, since I always tried developing the attitude of THINKING in English, which helped me with the correct expression in the English language. It is not only THINKING but also putting emotions into the expressions, which makes the communication most powerful and effective. This gave me an enhanced perspective since communicating in English was always found to be crisp, precise and easier too. Addressing the meetings, audience (larger or smaller) is observed to be more effective and simpler in English. However, at times, we need to maintain the regional language flavor as well, depending upon the forum. No communication can be complete and impactful without genuine emotions and expressions put into it.

With this personal experience, I also realized that people/professionals from our country—India are very particular and careful in speaking correct English and they do put in lots of efforts to ensure the accuracy in English they use—either verbal or written. And this precisely results in India being the most preferred country for many multinationals to come and start their business in India. In fact, multinational companies are able to source the best of the talent from India and are setting up their businesses like call centers, KPOs, BPOs, manufacturing units, etc. Many of the MNCs set up in India are catering to the markets across Asia, giving India the status of a corporate hub for the continent. And this is all possible primarily due to our flexibility to adapt to English effectively, despite the amazing diversity of languages existing in our culture-rich country.

So I can summarize that English is the language which is very effective for clear communication, understanding, resulting in economic growth of working individuals as well as of our country.

—Harish Nandwani,
Vice President—Human Resources,
Garware-Wall Ropes Ltd.

F. My proficiency in English has helped shape my life in many ways. As a Hmong American and former refugee from the Secret War in Laos, English is my second language. Although difficult for me to learn when I first came to the United States, knowledge of the English language has proven crucial to my success in American society. I could not have achieved the level of education I have obtained without having the ability to speak, read and write English. English has also been a vital tool for me in building friendships and connecting with others in my community.

—Ms. Mor Chang, MSW,
Social Worker, Founder and Editor of
Asian American Poetry Journal (USA)

G. The English language is the only language in which I write. Though I can speak in Kashmiri, Hindi and Urdu, but for writing I use English only, mainly because I have studied the language and feel comfortable with it.

I have been organizing workshops for Asian and Afro-Asian Writers since the 1970s at the India International Center as a Course Director. At these workshops I have invited the best editors and authors to speak to the participants. It made me to learn the craft of writing and editing. I have authored and edited more than fifty books. I still feel the language is global in scope and simple as a medium of expression. It has a great future. I get the best and latest books on the themes of my choice in English, which are not available in any other language, and now, in this computer age I find myself comfortable at accessing large databases that are available through the Web using the English font.

In no Indian language, except in English, you get the best courseware for students. The State governments and the Central governments have failed in developing the best and the latest textbooks for students in Indian languages. As a result the students studying through local languages are at a great disadvantage. They have only the degrees with them, and most of them cannot compete with students who excel studying through English medium.

—Dr. H.K. Kaul,
Founder of DELNET and Poetry Society of India,
Author, Library and Information Specialist, and
Institution Builder

H. English is a vital part of modern day society especially now with the Internet gaining more grounds, worldwide.

We don't realize how English has become such an essential part of global communication, apart from other languages such as Mandarin and Spanish coming to the fore.

If we didn't have the English language, I think we might get by but not as effectively as we'd hope.

I use English daily and it is a part of how I communicate with people as a crafts person and in the office and I very rarely have to use another language.

I can envisage a day when everyone uses English in the workplace and at home more so than now because it is used so widely—even in countries where English isn't spoken. Globally then and even locally, I can't foresee other languages overtaking English as the language most widely spoken.

—Ms. Colleen Lue (UK),
Businesswoman and Journal Editor

I. Left as a legacy by the colonizers but becoming a boon to us, English is not the language of any particular community in any province of India but a language popular in the whole of India; it has evolved replacing other languages, even pushing the claim of Hindi, as it could not capture the heart of all Indians. The only language, the real Indian cultural language acceptable to all Indians, as it belonged to none in particular, was Sanskrit but it could not forge ahead due to intervention of other languages and politics. English is the most accepted international language. It has become a literary and link language among all educated Indians.

I used to write in my own language, Bengali, but the circulation of the magazines was limited and here the literary grouping, monopoly and personal choices were pernicious to a good progress for all aspirants in literature. I find a tremendous scope in English through which I am linked not only to fellow Indians but all writers of the language throughout the world while continuing my bilingual character of writing in Bengali also. The scope of English has been widened through translations. It certainly forges all Indian minds together leading to better understanding and peace. It is the best peace-link among the people of the globe.

—Aju Mukhopadhyay,
Fiction Writer, Poet and Essayist

J. My mother is American born, so English was part of my daily life since I was a little boy.

I was born in Guatemala, Central America. My mother is an American, born in New Orleans, Louisiana, and she spoke English and Italian to us. My father, a career Diplomat, spoke German, English and Spanish, and my grandmother spoke Italian. So I have learned all of those languages plus, me and my brother were sent to a French boarding school for three years and I also speak and write French.

I made a point to learn English as perfect as possible for many reasons.

I always loved the United States very much so and what the country represents: Freedom, Equal Opportunities, a true Democracy and all the possibilities that it offers in business being the largest economy in the world. Not to become wealthy myself, but to make enough money to be able to help others.

In 1977, I decided to move to United States to pursue a career in the film business. I wanted to produce moving pictures. Years educating myself in such a fascinating trade, I realized a good screenplay was needed to make a good film so I had to "really" learn the English language and became a screenwriter.

I took paper, pencil and a dictionary and started copying magazine articles. After about a year of doing it for one hour every day, I was speaking and writing

English like if I had a Major degree in English Literature, which I am very proud of. All self taught.

—Juan Rudeke,
Managing Director, World Peace Organization (USA)

K. I owe a great deal to my teachers in English, right from elementary school to Master's program in English literature. They were dedicated teachers, who enjoyed their chosen vocation. One of my teachers advised us to keep a dictionary always handy. I have one by my bedside, and one on my writing desk. Proficiency in the language helps me in understanding different cultures. English is a global language. Having lived in Kashmir and down south in Chennai, USA and Europe, the language barrier was sort of overcome due to the ability to converse in English. What better way to learn about culture, people and land. It helped me as a writer, poet, teacher and journalist. When people from different parts of my country come under one platform, the language helps in breaking barriers. Whenever I attend poetry meets, we are able to connect through the medium of this language. After all, a writer writes first due to some inner compulsion to write for self-expression and exploration, and then to make human connection. With just a paper and pen, a writer's equipment, or through Internet, I am able to connect worldwide. It gives me immense pleasure, a sense of fulfillment and creative satisfaction. Thanks to my parents, who were farsighted enough to send me to a school, where the medium of instruction was English.

—Ms. Mamta Agarwal,
Writer, Journalist, Poet, and
Member of FOSWAL and Indian Society of Authors

L. English has helped me to build a wide communication with other poets, editors, and people around the world. A survey conducted some time back stated that one-fourth of the entire world now speaks English. It is the universal language of commerce and airlines. The widespread knowledge of English has helped me to get my poetry and stories into print in 24 countries. It has also enabled me to read many foreign writers whose work has now been translated into English. Without English, I would not have gained all the knowledge of literature, history, and philosophy from around the world or been able to share their thoughts and mine for a united struggle for peace among men. The contacts have broadened my knowledge and helped me to build so many wonderful friendships. English has brought me into the brotherhood of man and helped to spread the message of world peace and universal harmony.

—Ms. Ruth Wildes Schuler,
American Poet and Author

M. The use of the English language is very important to me in so many ways.

Firstly, being born in England and having English as my native language, has given me the tool to be able to communicate with people around the world, as it is the most universal language used today. I find this very beneficial both as the editor of an International poetry magazine, and for my own personal use as a writer. I especially love English in a poetic sense, as it is a rich and fruitful language, thus making it perfect to obtain depth and beauty.

I love the older dialect of English, which I feel worked beautifully with the classic writers and poets such as Shakespeare. There was a natural elegance to the old English language which worked perfectly.

The English language is soulful and beautiful. I just hope this richness can remain within the language of today, even if, just in a poetic sense.

—Ms. Lisa Deer,
Editor of *Decanto Journal* and Writer (UK)

APPENDICES

Appendix 1—Good to Know Acronyms

ADVT — Need I tell you the full form? I will give it to anyway, it is Advertisement.

AGL — Above Ground Level (This one is a must to have a safe plane landing.)

AI — Artificial Intelligence

B2B — Business to Business Transactions

CV — Curriculum Vitae (Something that we all update from time to time.)

DD — Demand Draft (How can we forget this one, we use it so often.)

ELT — English Language Teaching

ESL — English as a Second Language

ESP — English for Special Purposes

FYI — For Your Information (Remember your first e-mail?)

GWTH — Growth

HQ — Head Quarters

I.E. — That is

IELTS — International English Language Testing System

JIT — Just in Time (This one has a universal appeal.)

KET — Key English Test

MBA — Master of Business Administration (Who doesn't want to be one!)

N/A — Not Applicable

OK — Okay (A ubiquitous word.)

POV — Point of View (What is your POV on life's challenges?)

ROI — Return on Investment

SWOT — Strengths, Weaknesses, Opportunities and Threats

TEA — Test of English for Aviation

TEFL — Teaching English as a Foreign Language

TESL — Teaching English as a Second Language

TOEFL — Test of English as a Foreign Language

USP — Unique Selling Point

VP — Vice President (A dream post!)

WALL — Web-Assisted Language Learning (A must know for all the tech-savvy learners of English.)

ZBA — Zero Balance Account (has a lot of advantages)

Did I miss any? Oh yes, I have missed hundreds of them, even more! My main aim is to help you realize that knowing the acronyms used in your profession will prevent you from falling into a whirlpool of problems.

Appendix 2—English Language Resources

I am not recommending or endorsing any of these resources. All I am trying to do is getting you started on the road to learning English. This is not an exhaustive list but just a snapshot of the various learning courses, material and other language-related resources available.

A. British Council is a premier institute that offers courses for both students and professionals. Enhance Your English in all aspects with the help of

http://www.britishcouncilonline.org

B. Online dictionary resources from Oxford University Press http://www.askoxford.com

C. Comprehensive language courses for pilots, air traffic controllers, mechanics and ground staff http://www.macmillanenglish.com/aviationenglish/index.html

D. Words used in BBC news reports http://www.bbc.co.uk/worldservice/learningenglish/language/wordsinthenews

E. For information on the varieties of English, visit the following website http://www.uni-due.de/SVE

F. CNN glossary of Business English terms http://money.cnn.com/services/glossary/a.html

G. Foundation Courses for English communication skills are offered in St. Xavier's College, Mumbai.

Appendix 3—References

Cotton, K. & Wikelund, K.R. (2007). Parent Involvement in Education. School Improvement Research Series (ED 285895).

Macmillan English Dictionary for Advanced Learners. 2002. Macmillan Education.

Roemer, T. (2010). *Education is the key to success, says US envoy*. India: *Sakaal Times*. 13 May, p. 3.

Swales, J. (1987). Utilizing the literatures in teaching the research paper. *TESOL Quarterly*, 21, pp. 41-68.

The Economist (1996) Language and Electronics: The coming global tongue. 21 December, pp. 37-39.

Index